ROCK PROGRESIVO

Partituras para aficionados al piano

MA
NON
TROPPO

© 2022, Miguel Ángel Fernández Pérez

© 2022, Redbook Ediciones, s. l., Barcelona

Diseño de cubierta: Regina Richling

ISBN: 978-84-18703-25-6

Depósito legal: B-1270-2022

Impreso por Ulzama, Pol. Ind. Areta, calle A-33, 31620 Huarte (Navarra)

Impreso en España - *Printed in Spain*

ROCK PROGRESIVO

Partituras para aficionados al piano

ROCK PROGRESIVO

Partituras para aficionados al piano

Catherine Howard

RICK WAKEMAN

A Whiter Shade of Pale

PROCOL HARUM

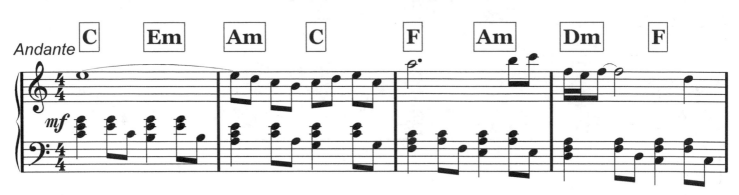

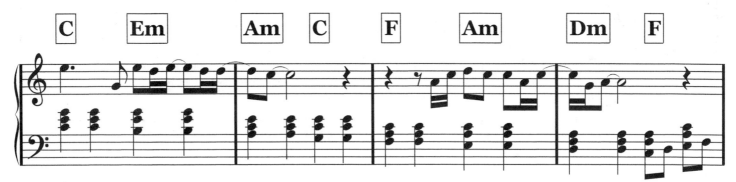

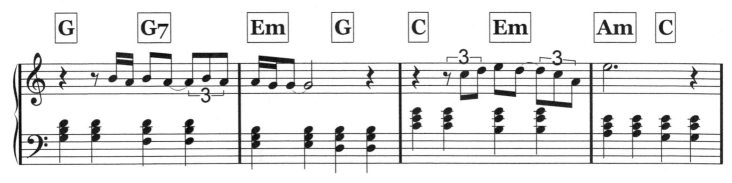

Colour My World

CHICAGO

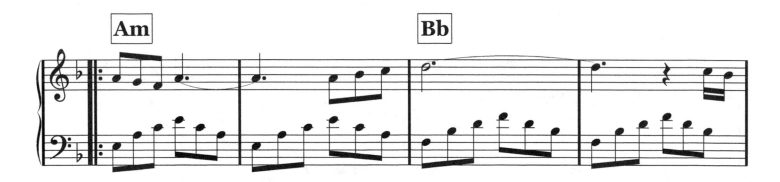

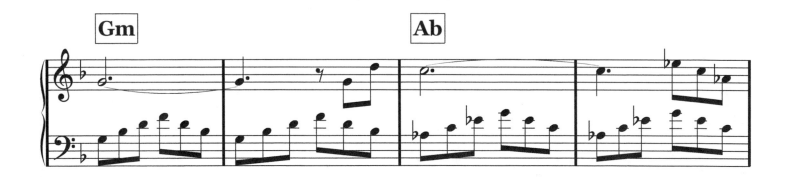

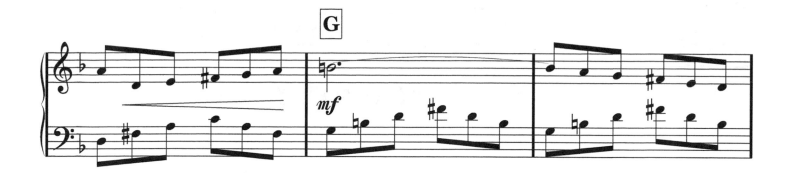

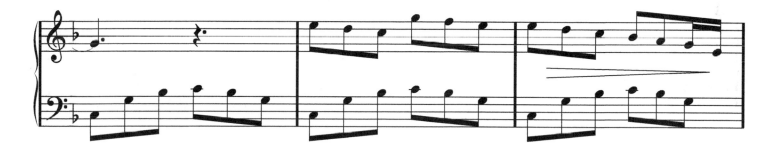

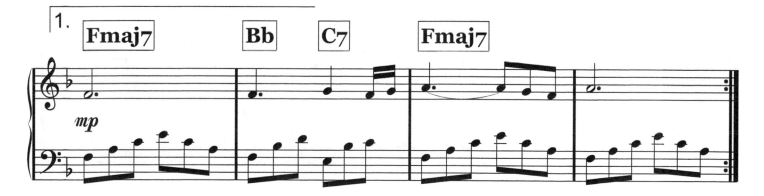

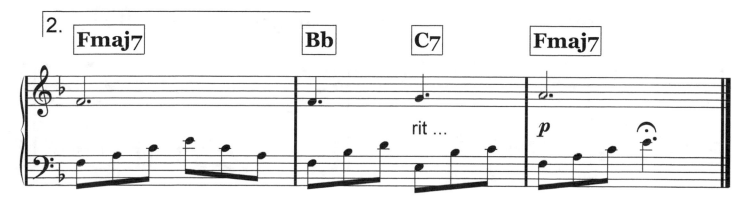

Horizons

STEVE HACKETT

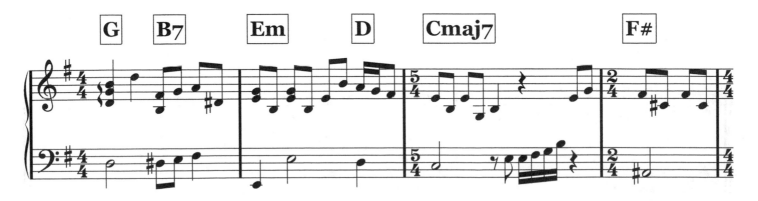

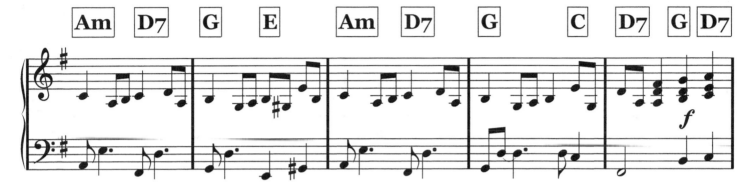

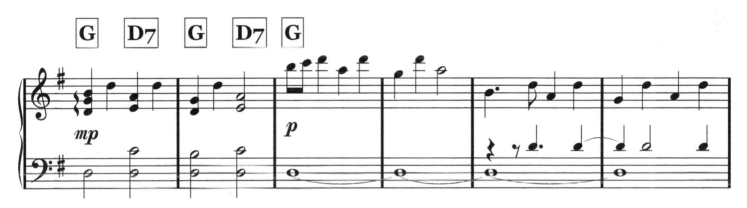

Peter Gunn

EMERSON, LAKE & PALMER

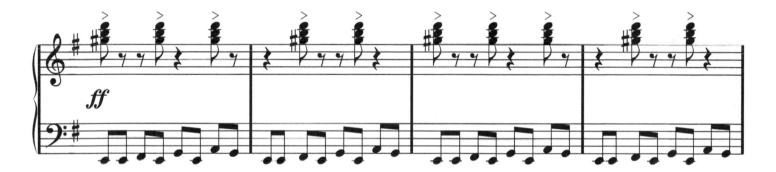

Ommadawn

MIKE OLDFIELD

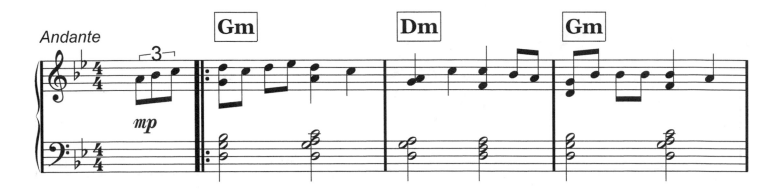

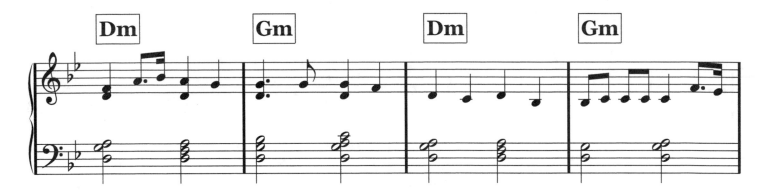

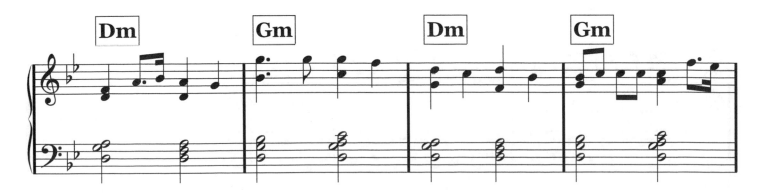

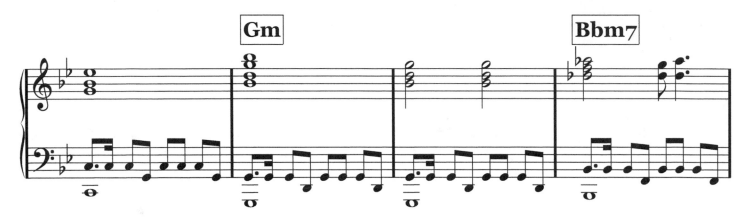

Spirit of the Water

CAMEL

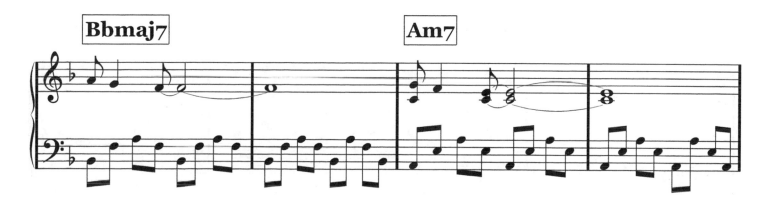

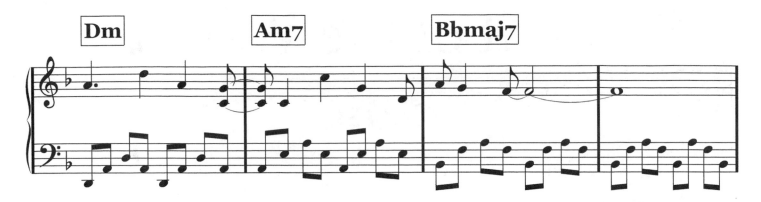

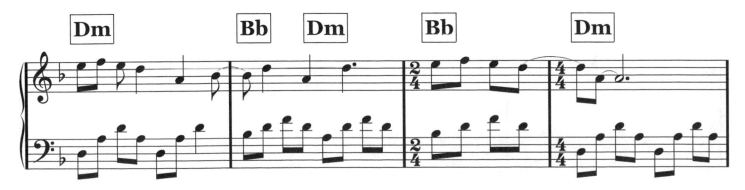

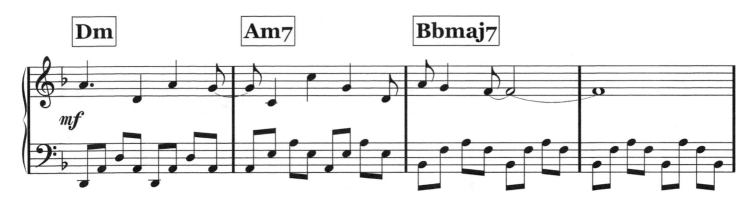

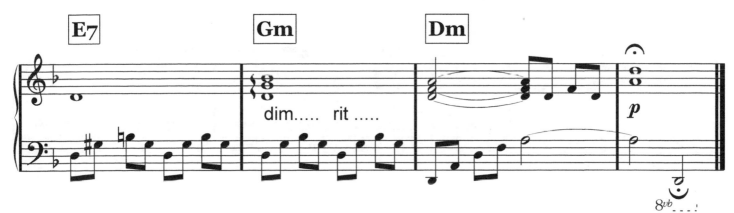

The Happiest Days of Our Lives
Another Brick in the Wall

PINK FLOYD

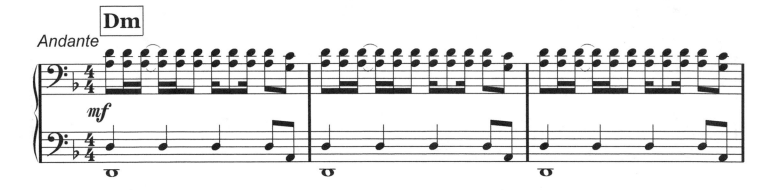

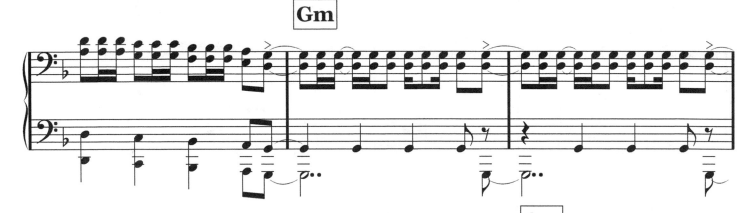

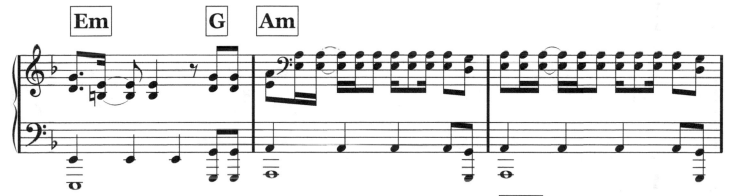

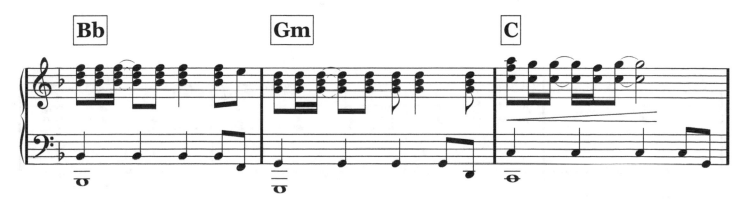

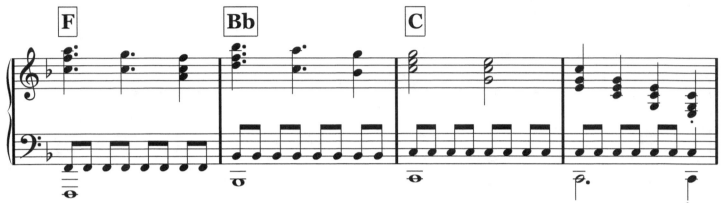

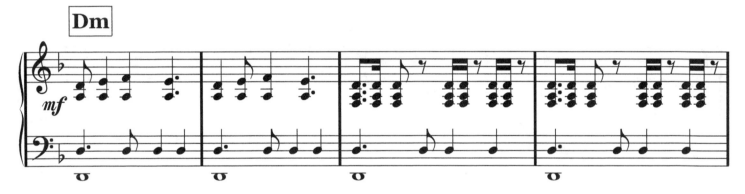

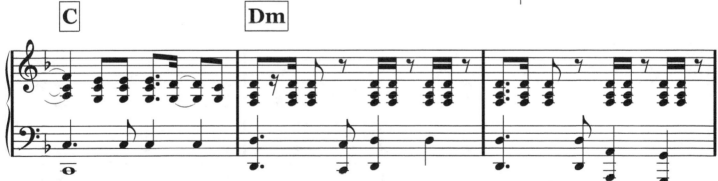

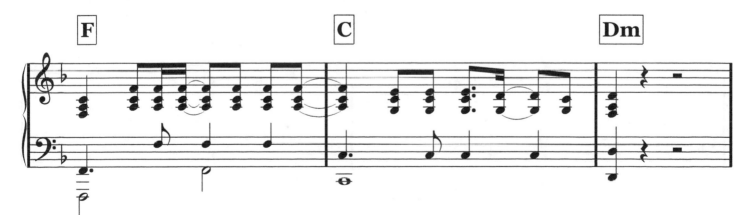

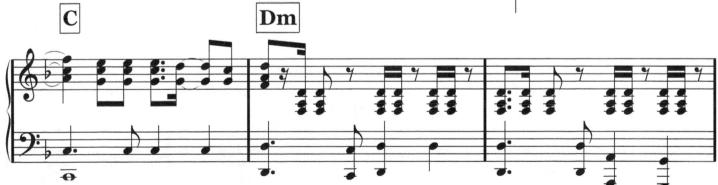

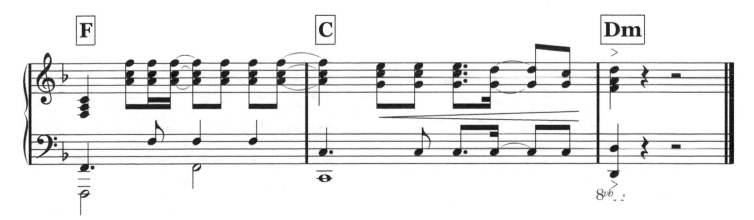

Sirius
Eye in the Sky

THE ALAN PARSONS PROJECT

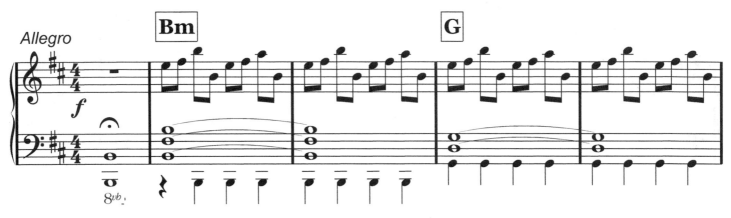

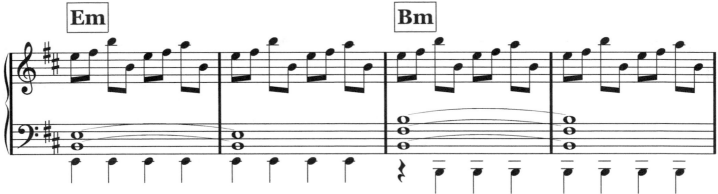

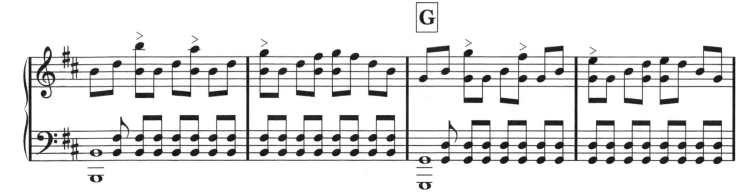

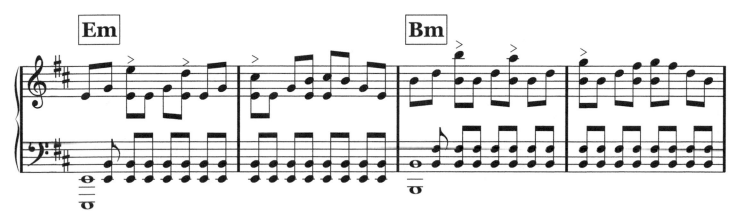

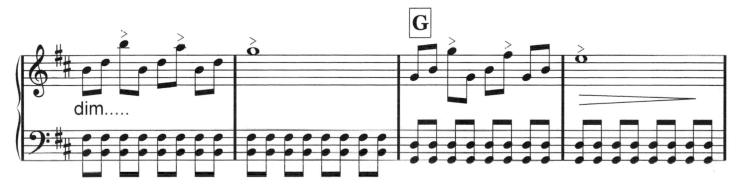

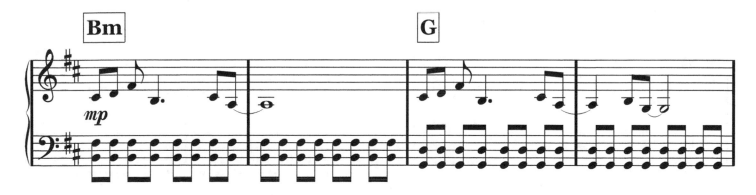

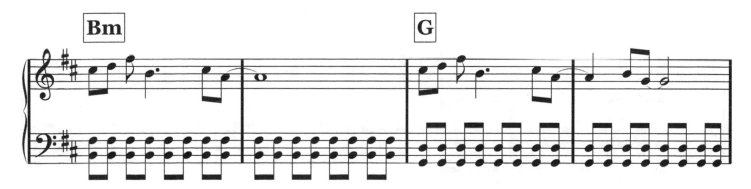

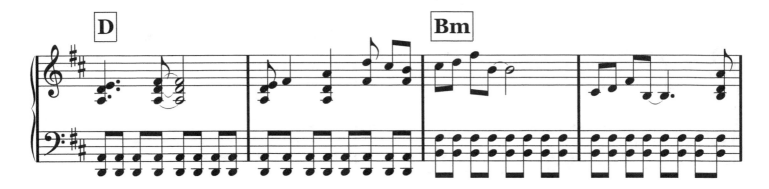

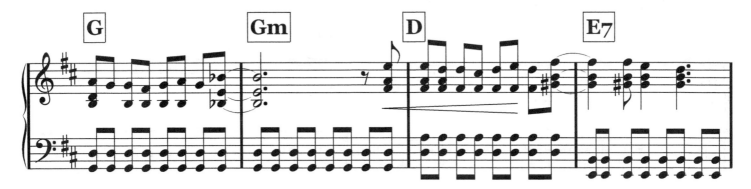

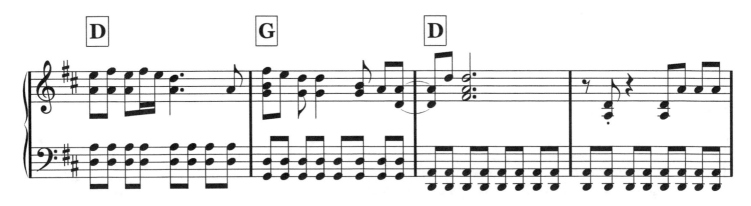

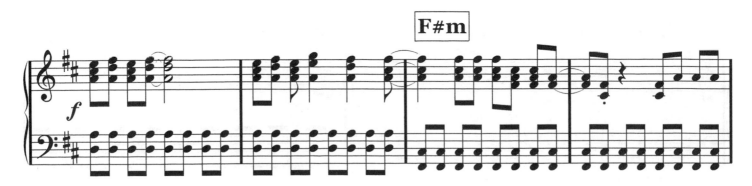

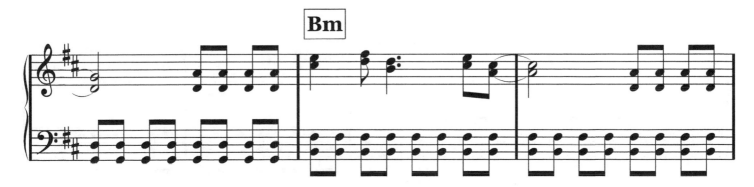

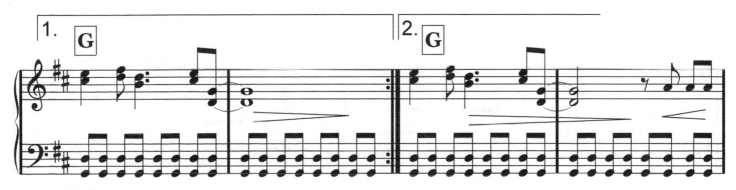

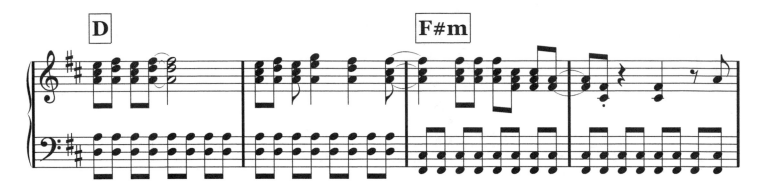

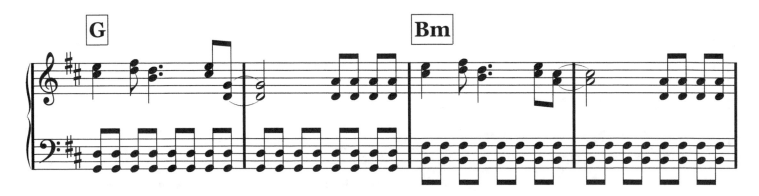

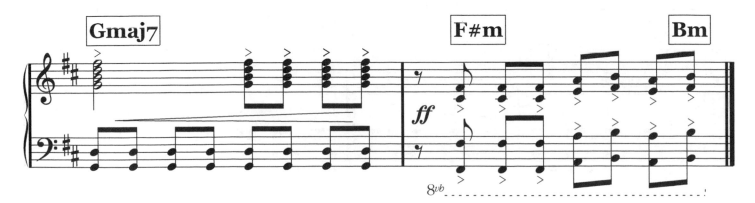

That´s All

GENESIS

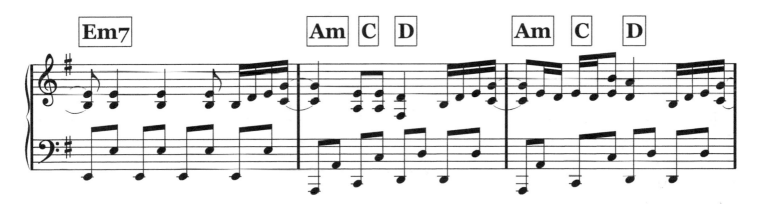

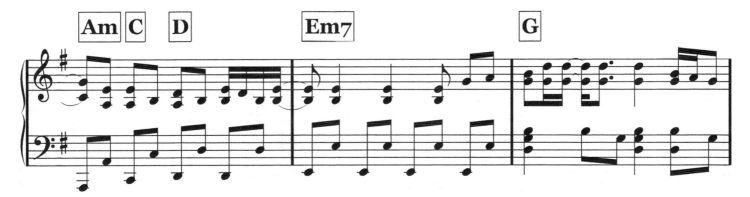

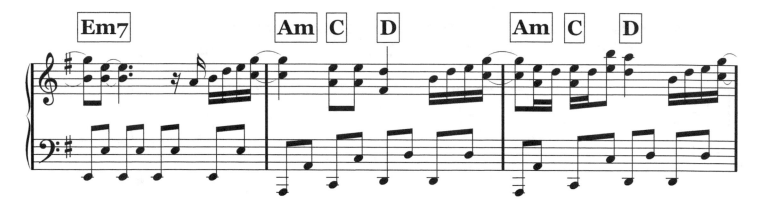

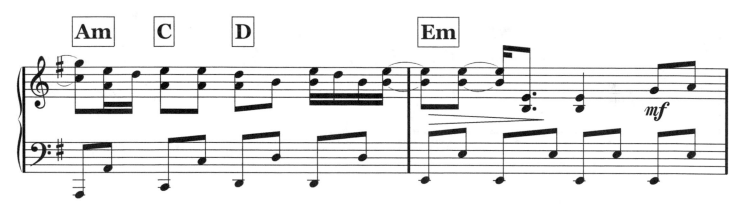

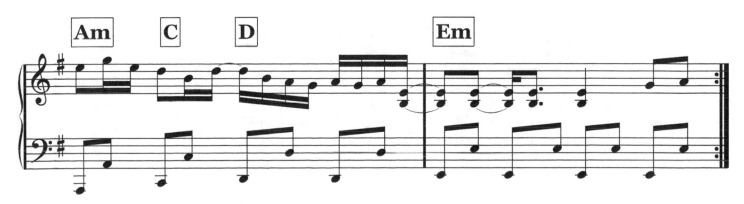

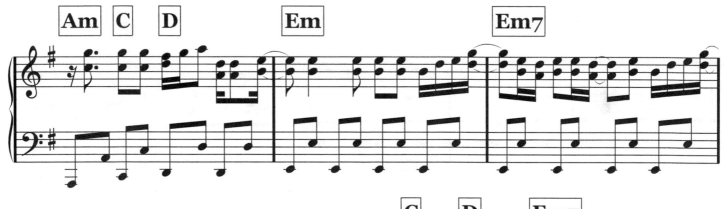

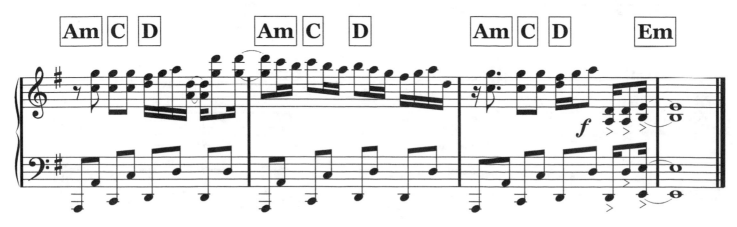

Heart of Lothian

MARILLION

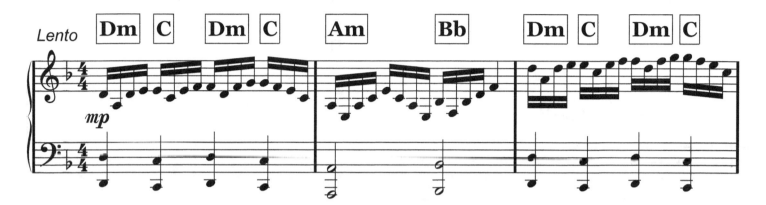

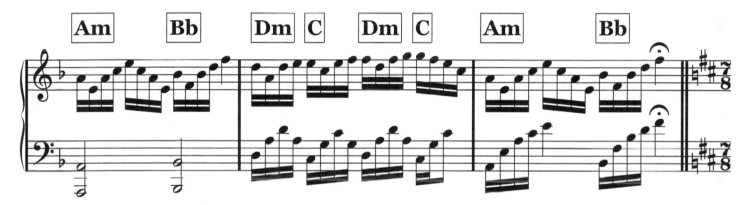

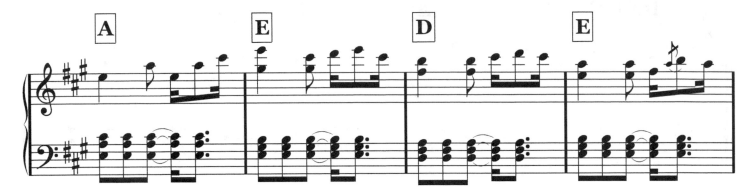

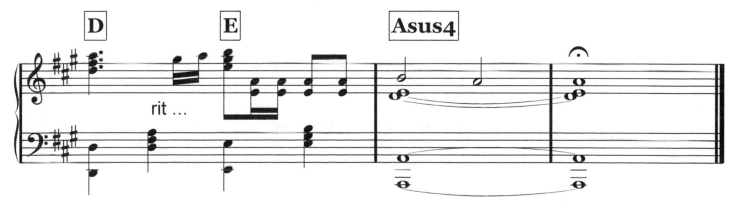

Hide in Your Shell

SUPERTRAMP

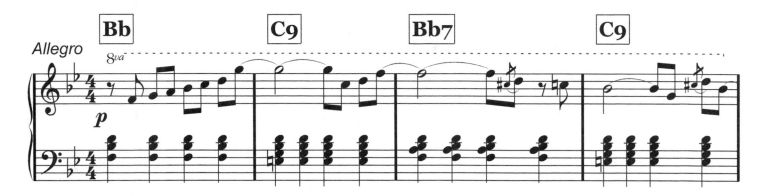

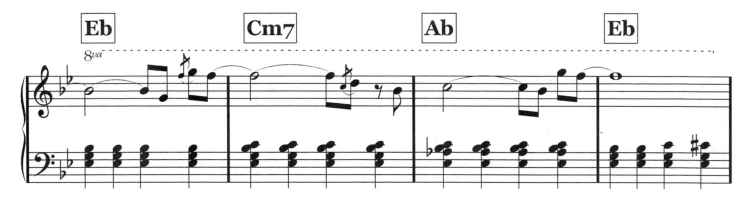

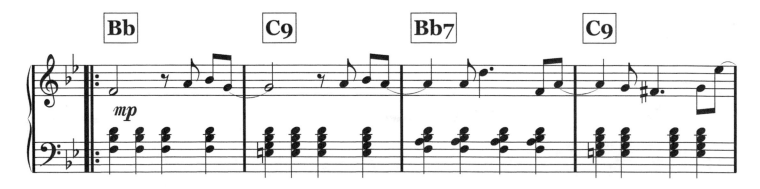

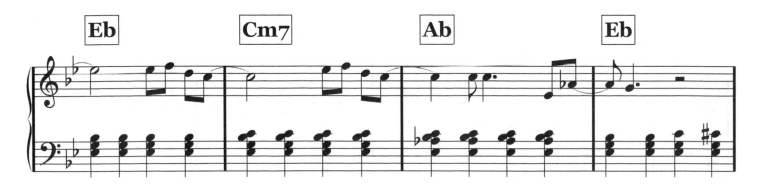

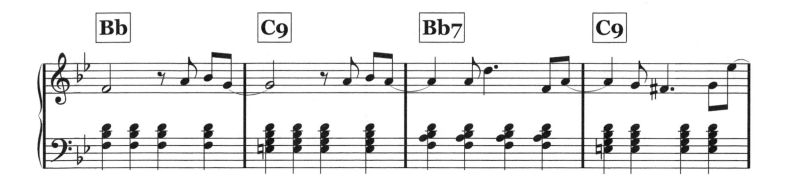

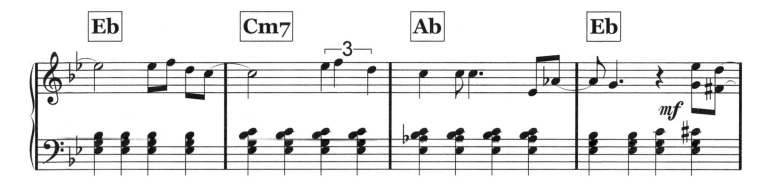

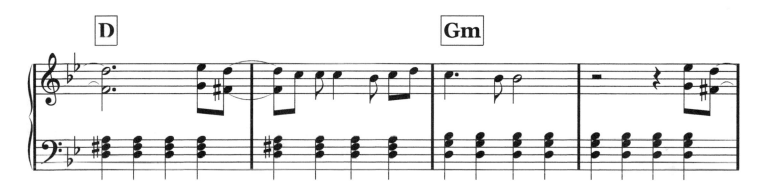

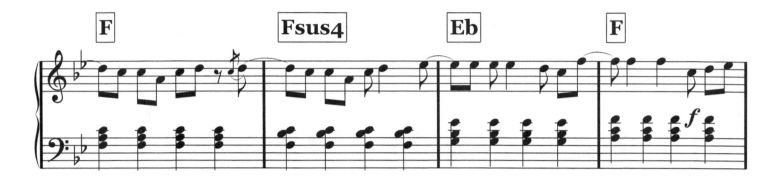

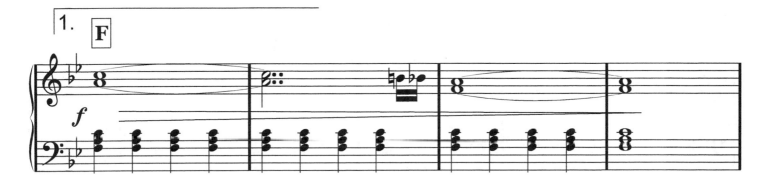

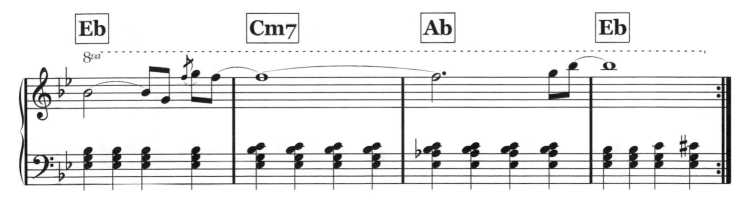

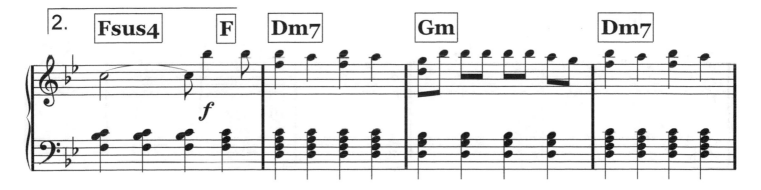

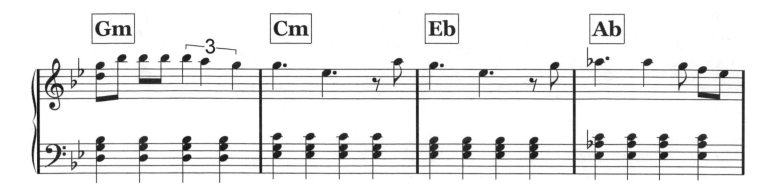

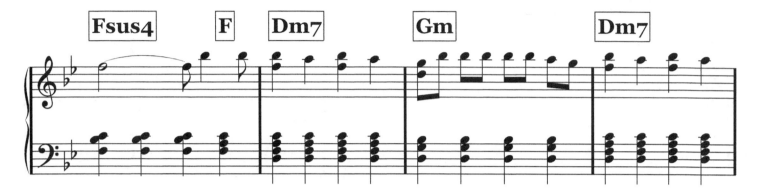

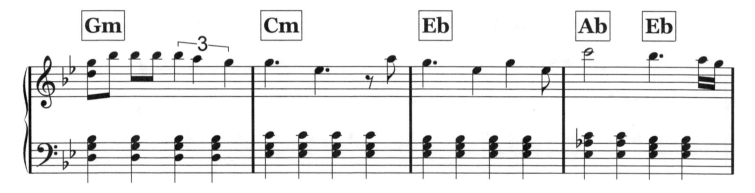

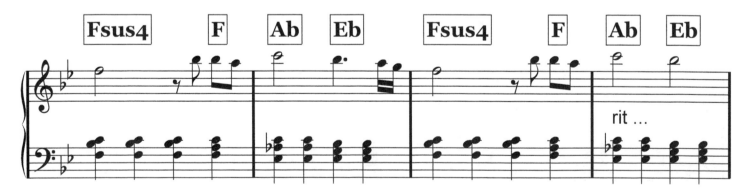

The Top of the Morning

MIKE OLDFIELD

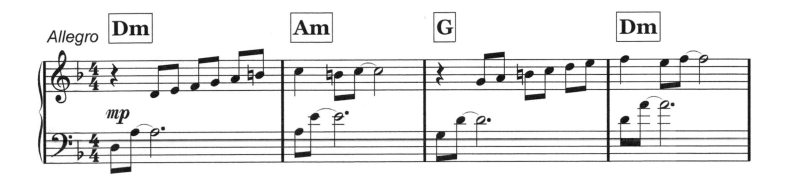

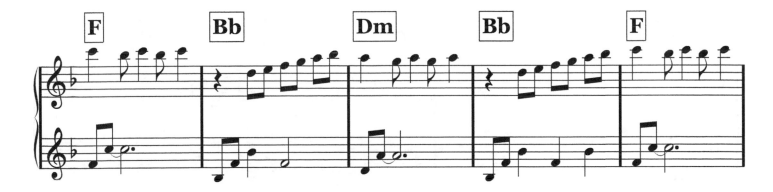

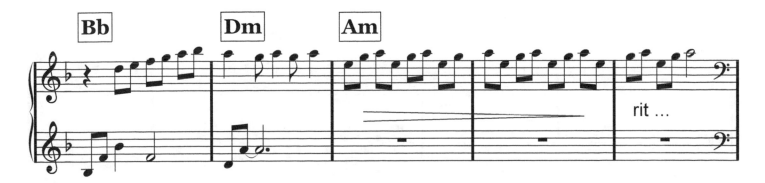

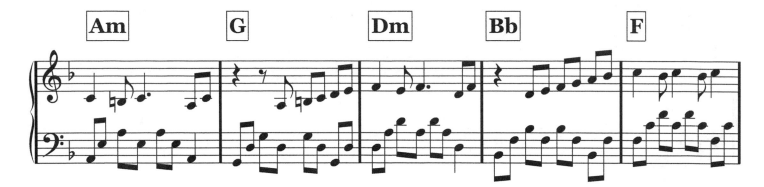

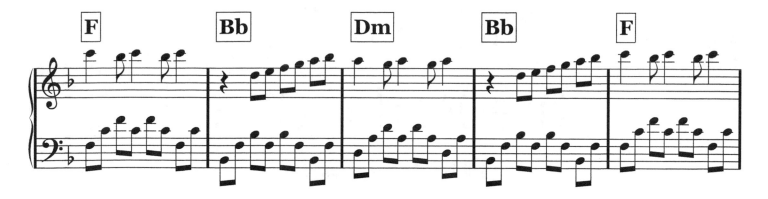

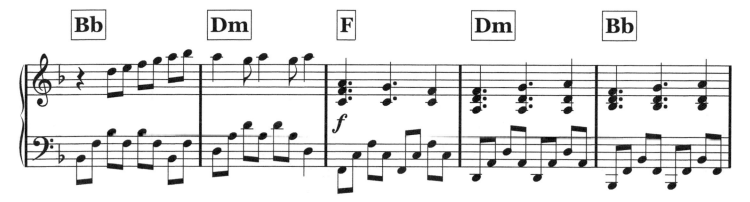

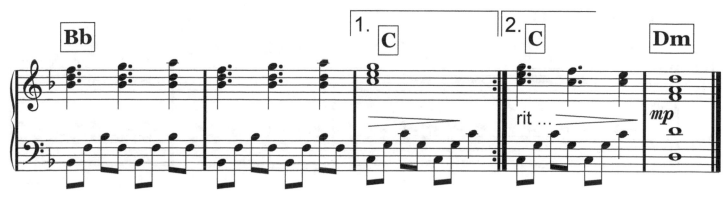

Video Killed the Radio Star

THE BUGGLES

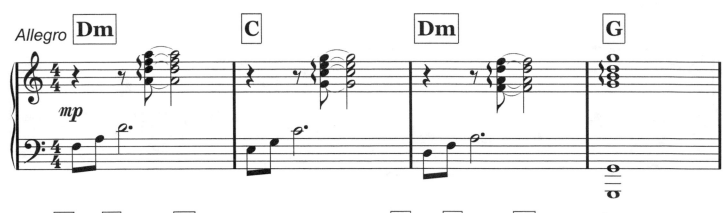

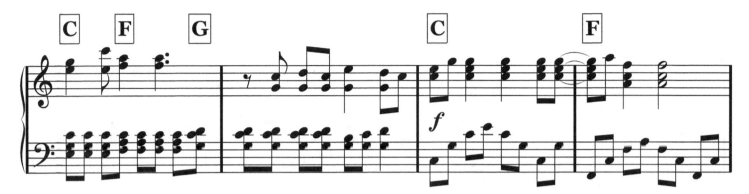

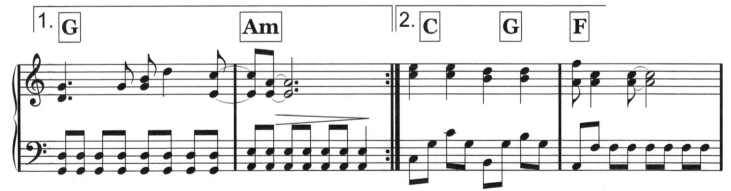

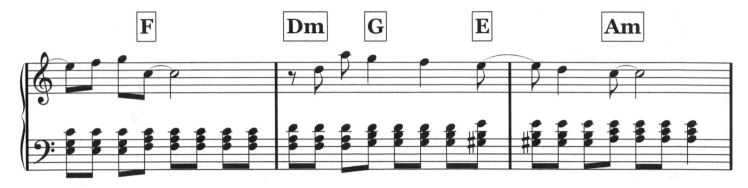

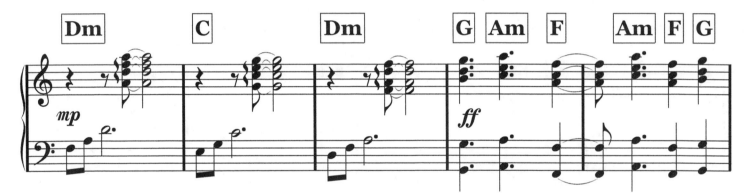

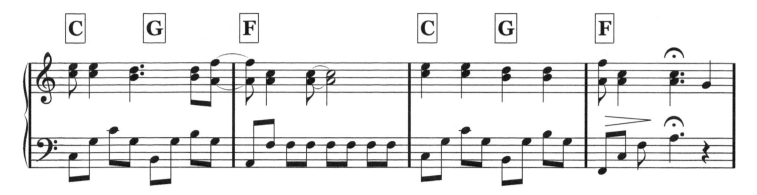

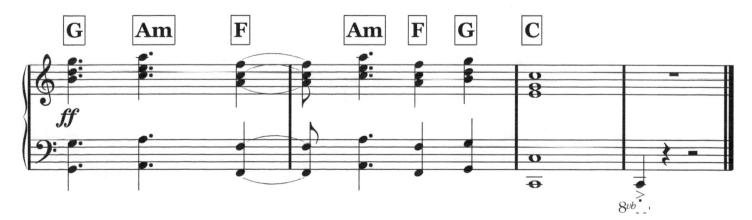

I've Seen All Good People

YES

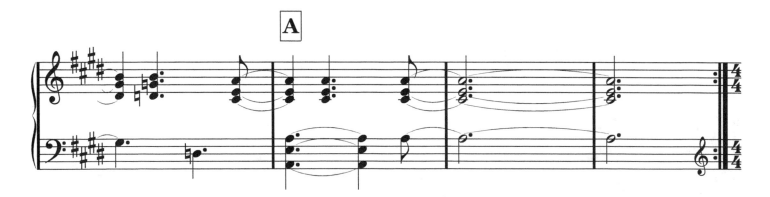

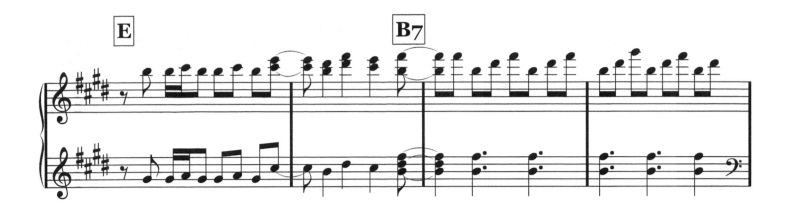

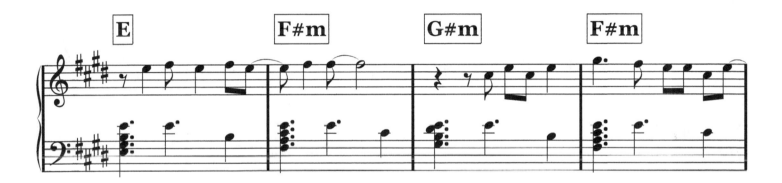

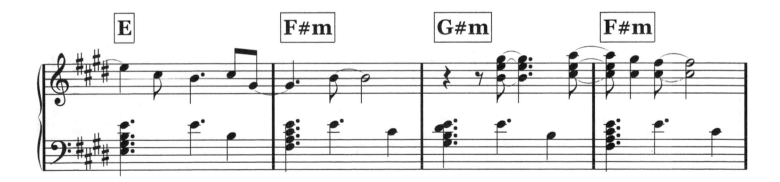

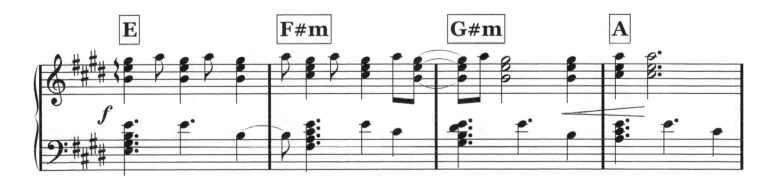

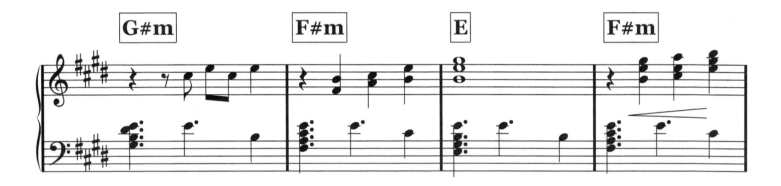

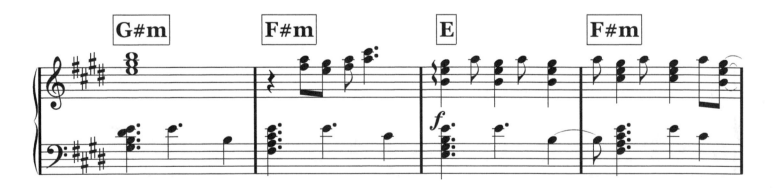

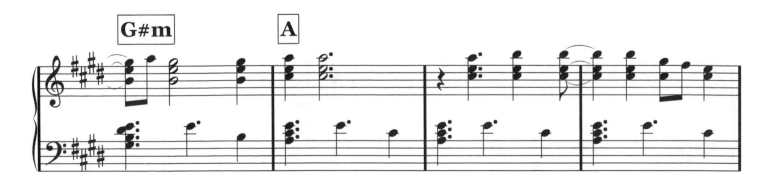

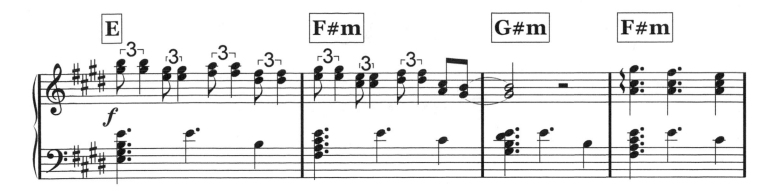

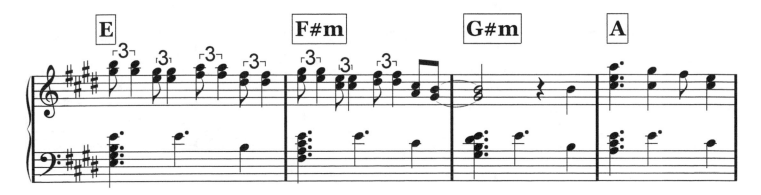

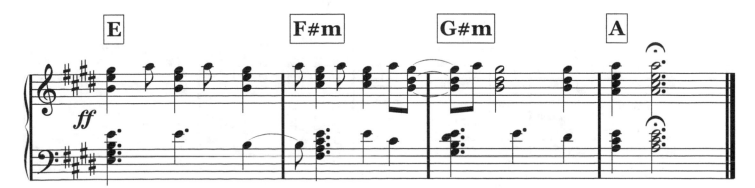

Wish You Were Here

PINK FLOYD

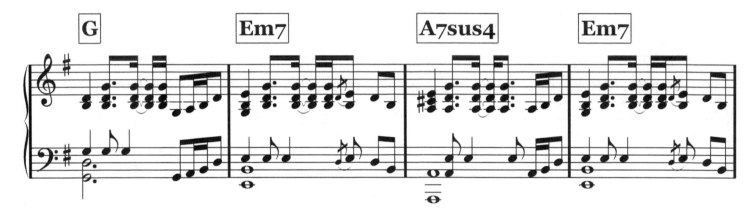

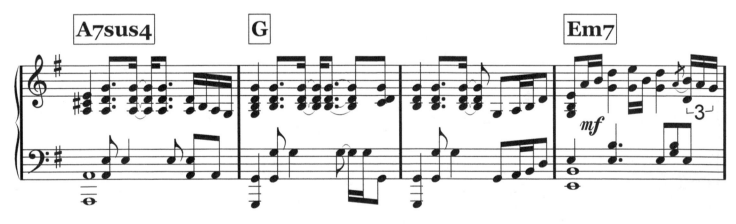

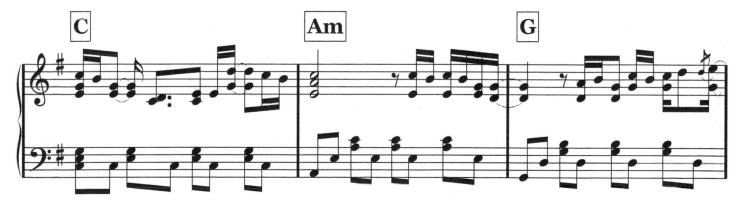

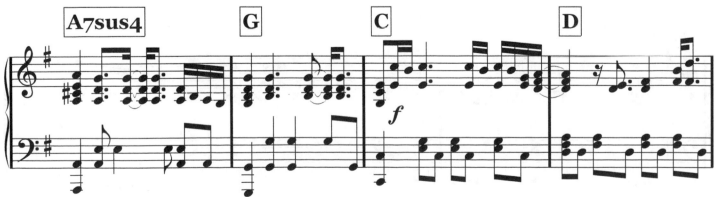

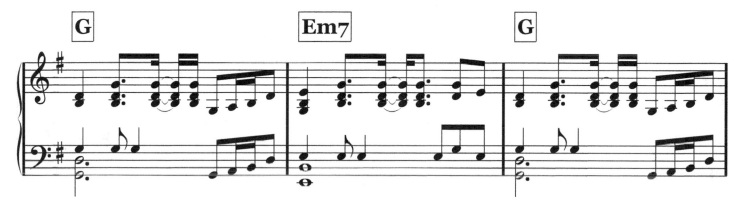

Rhayader

CAMEL

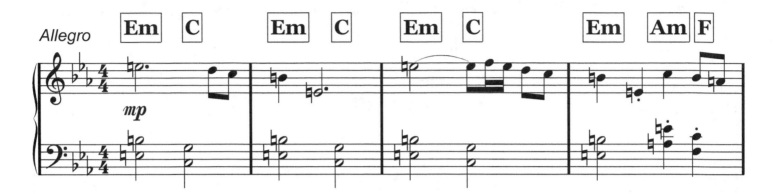

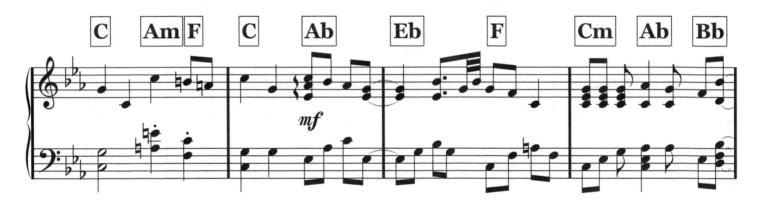

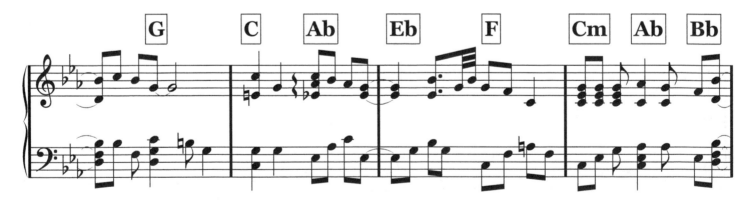

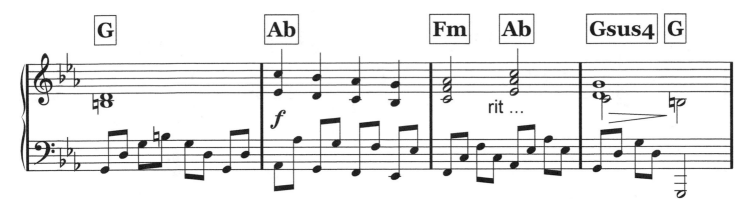

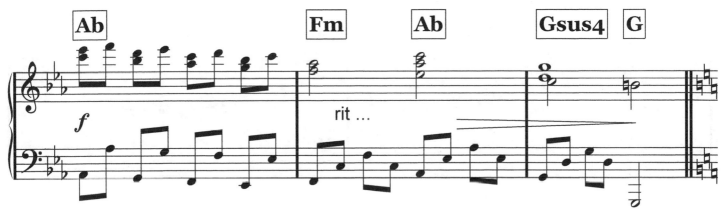

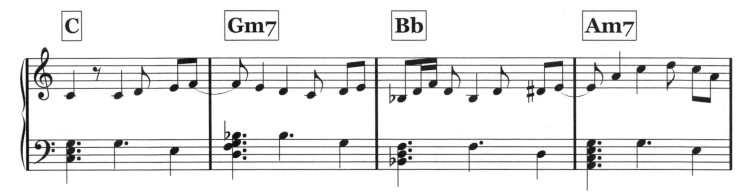

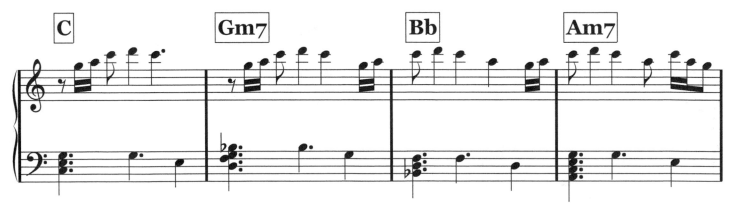

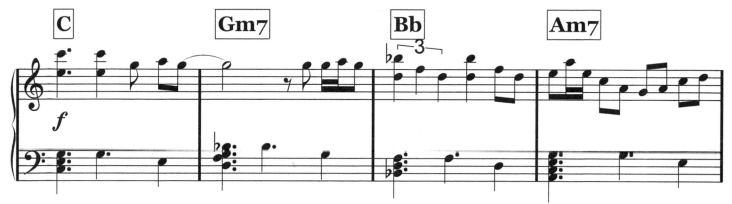

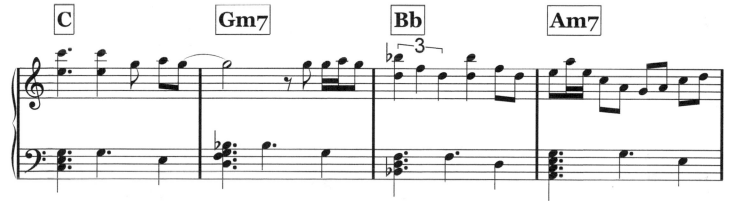

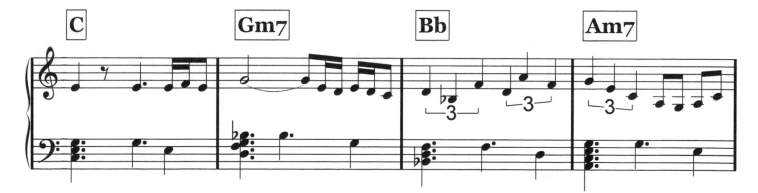

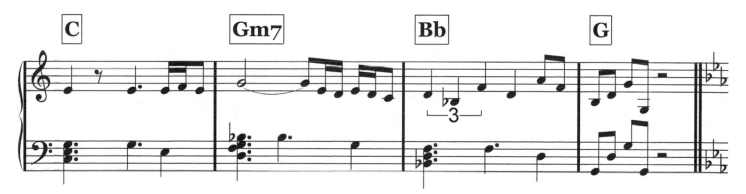

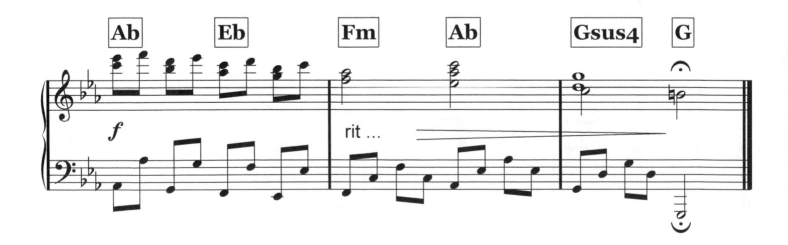

Sentinel

MIKE OLDFIELD

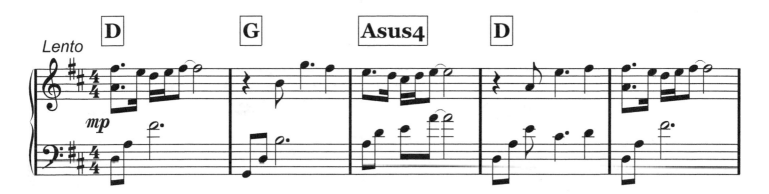

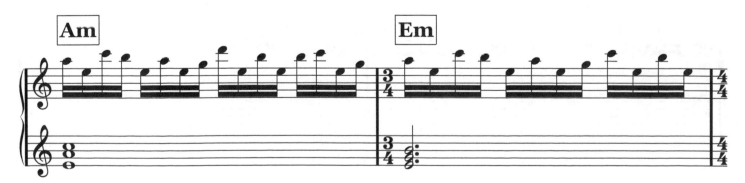

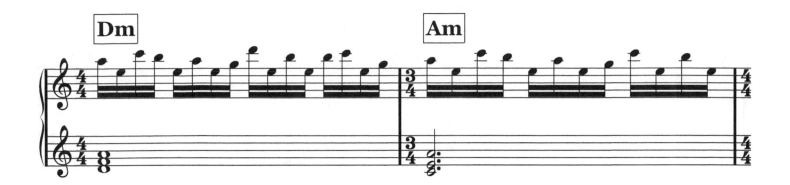

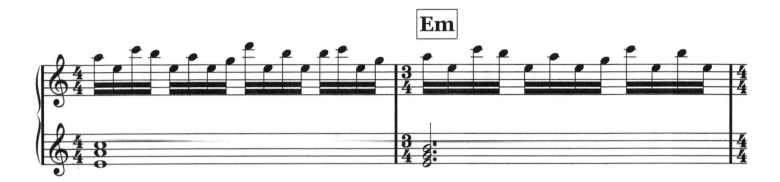

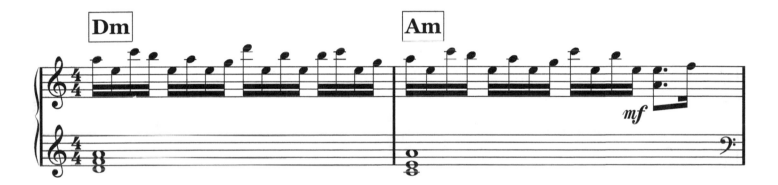

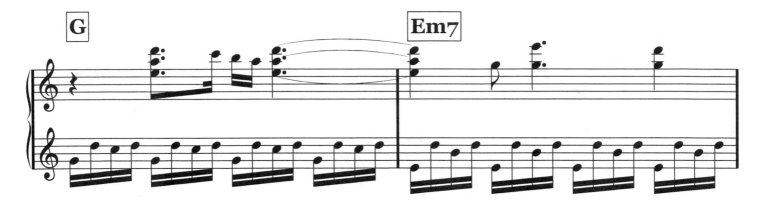

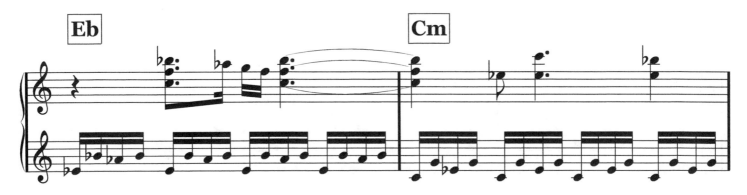

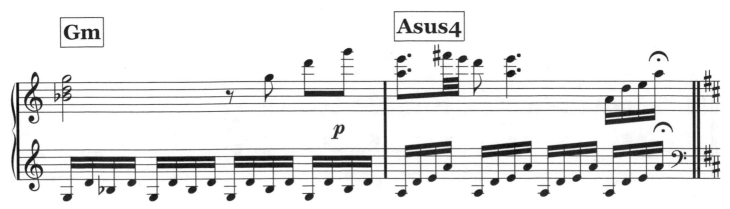

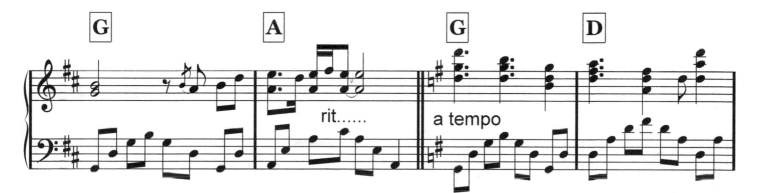

rit......   a tempo

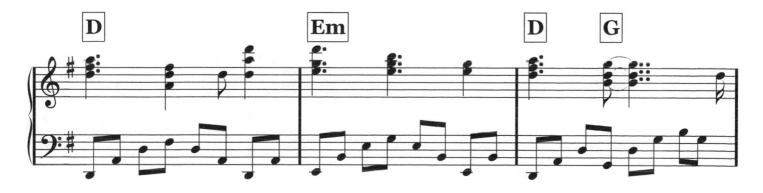

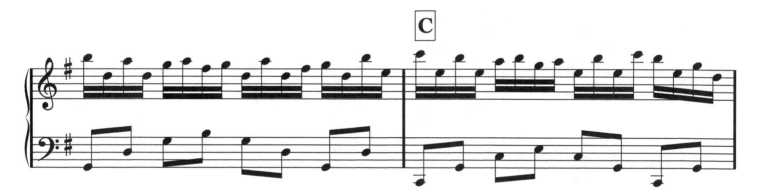

Too Old to Rock 'n' Roll: Too Young to Die!

JETHRO TULL

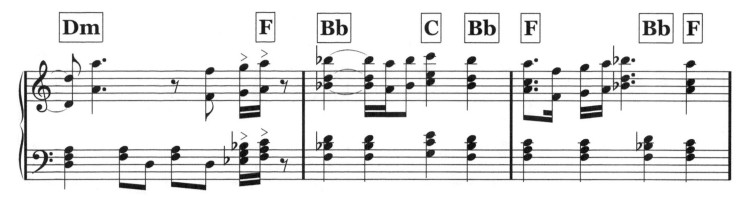

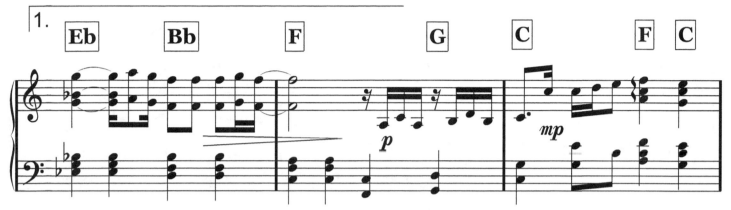

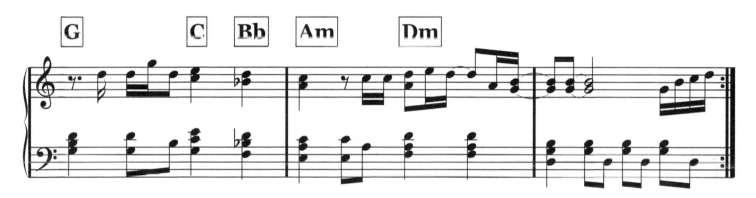

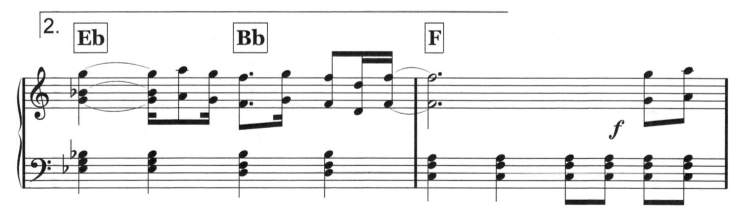

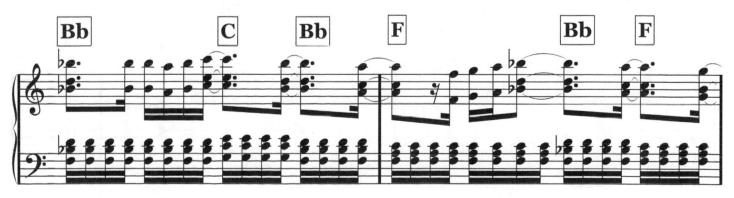

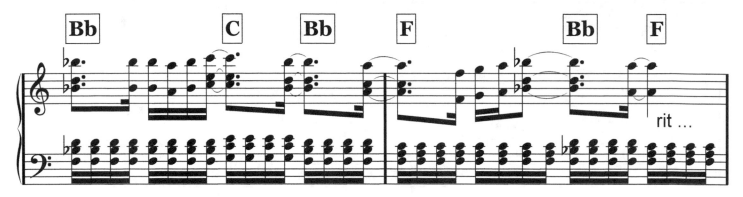

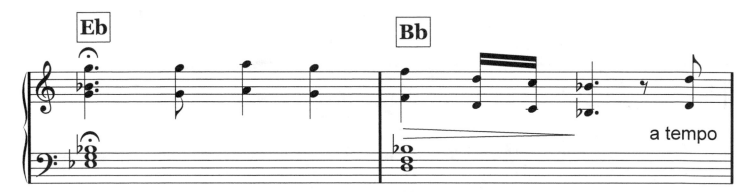

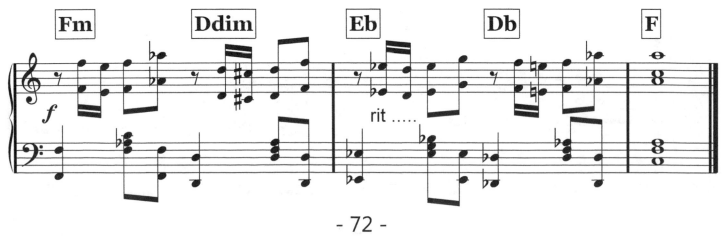

El hijo del alba

BLOQUE

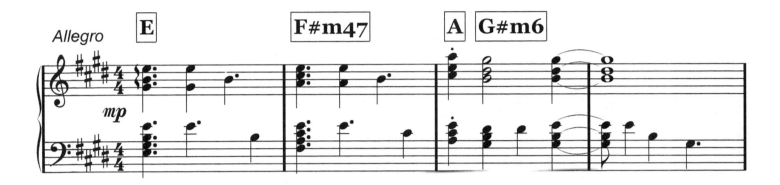

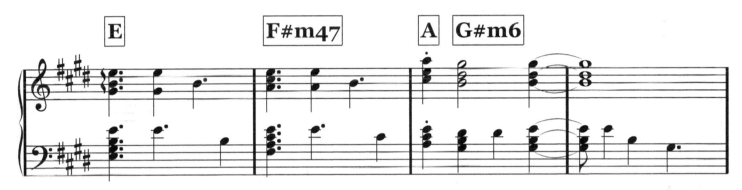

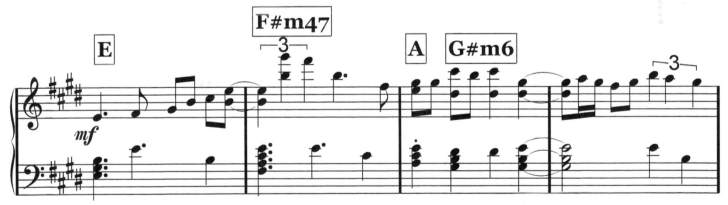

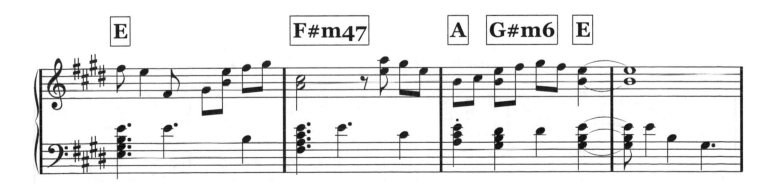

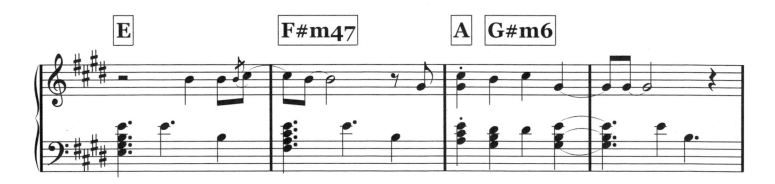

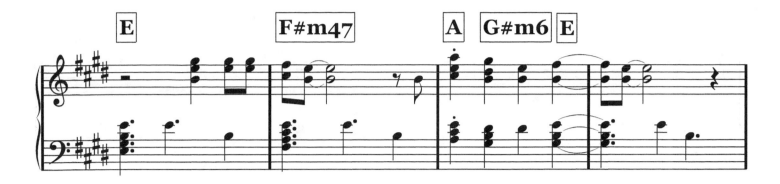

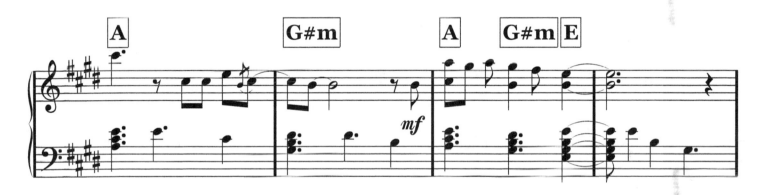

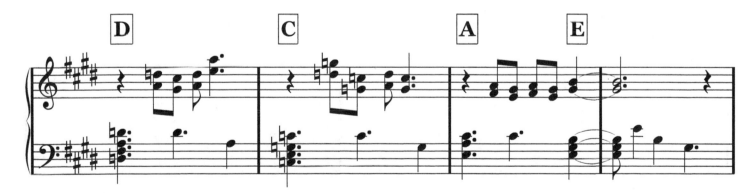

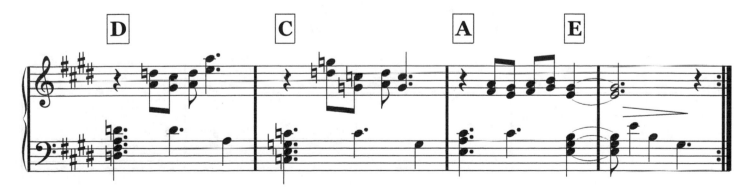

- 75 -

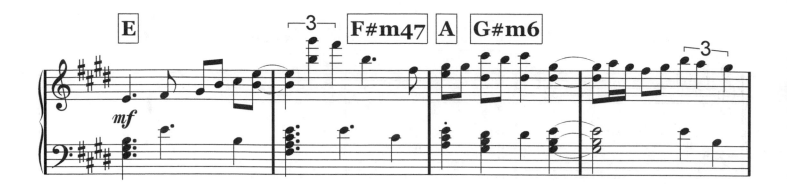

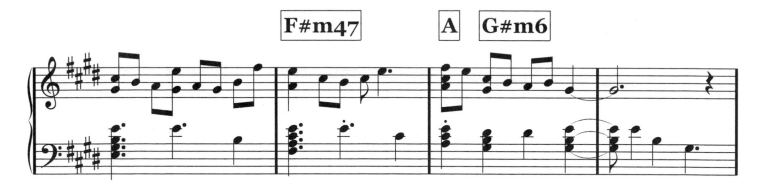

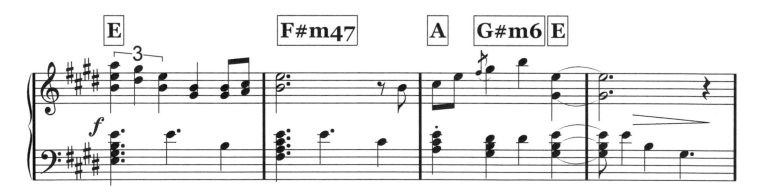

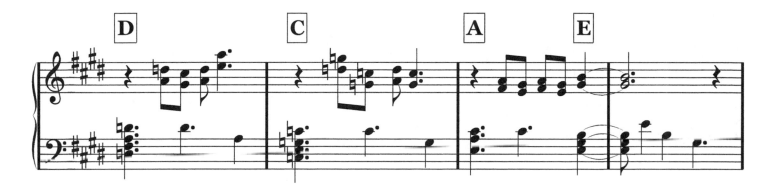

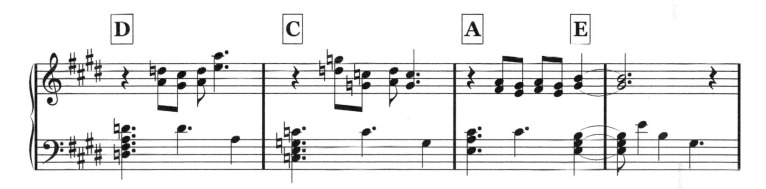

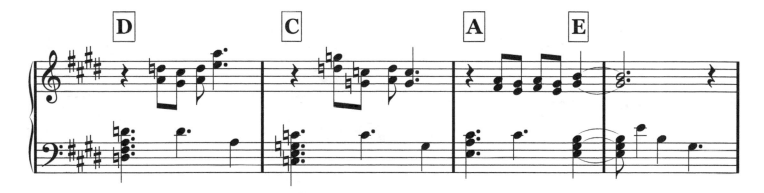

Don´t Give Up

PETER GABRIEL

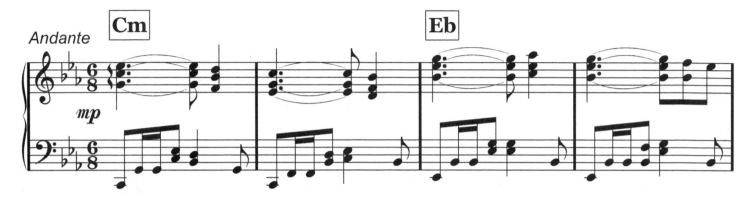

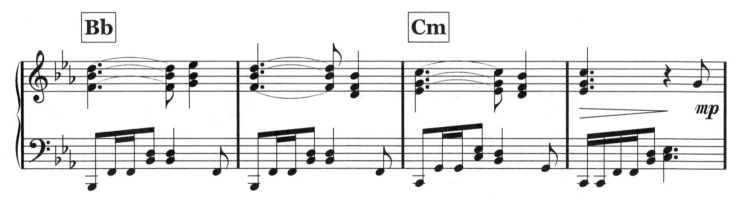

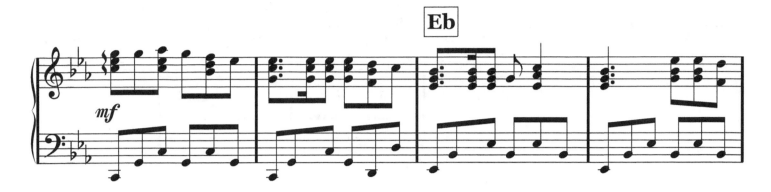

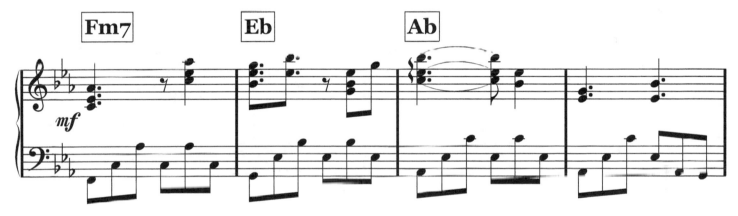

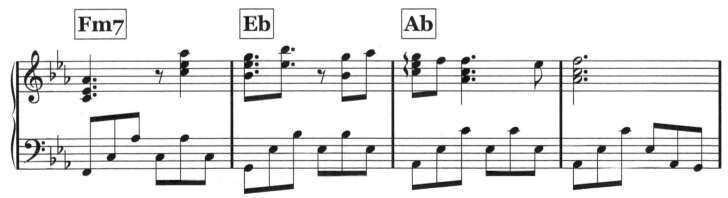

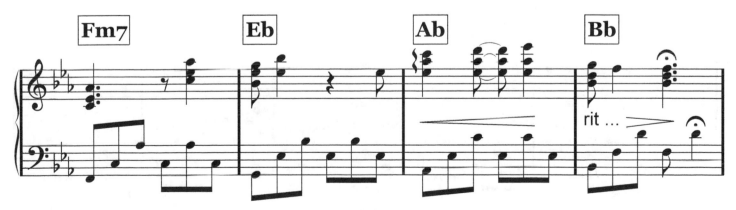

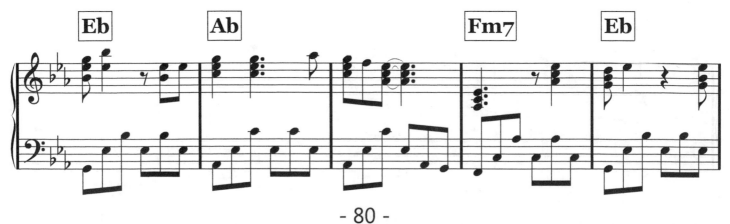

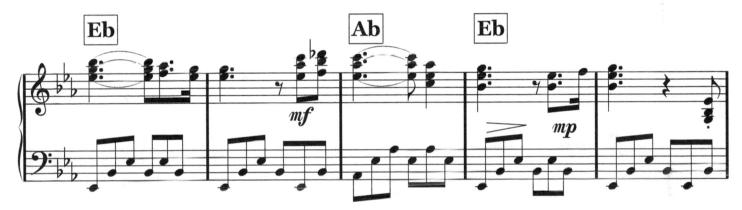

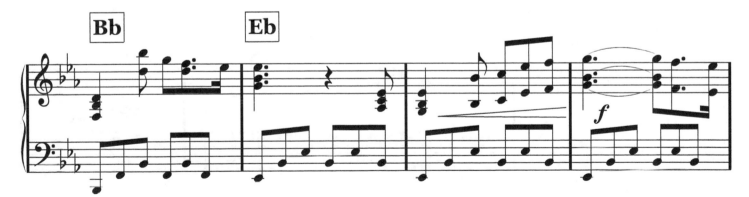

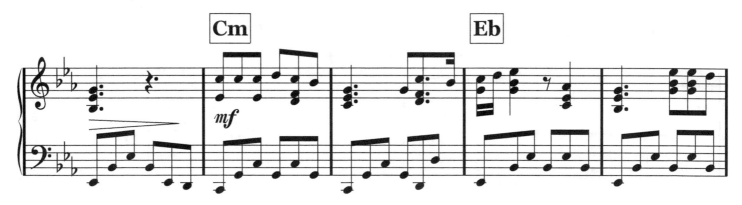

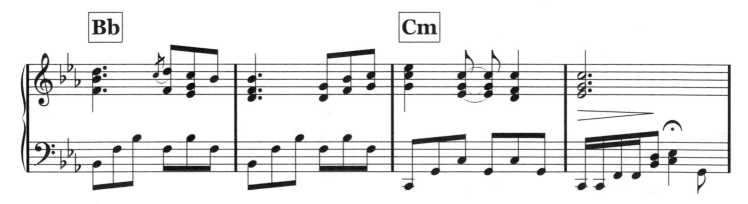

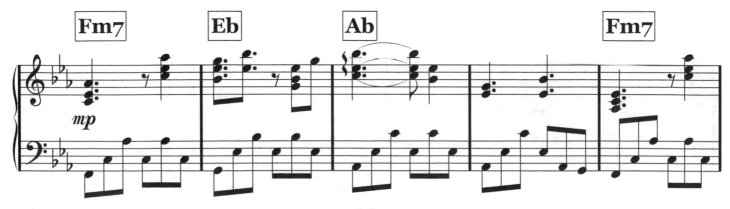

Lord Is It Mine

SUPERTRAMP

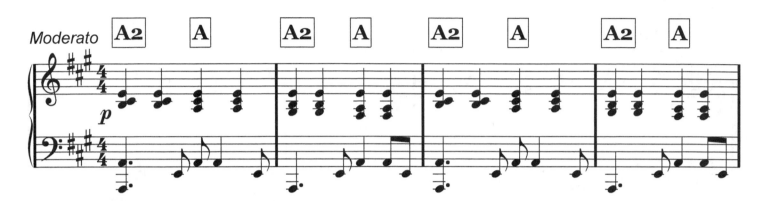

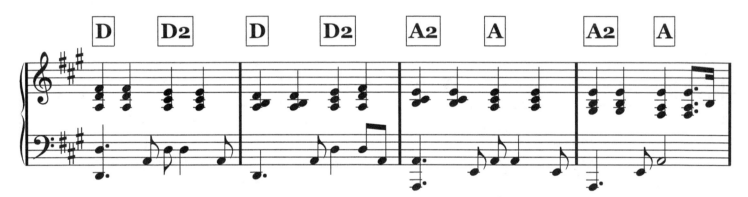

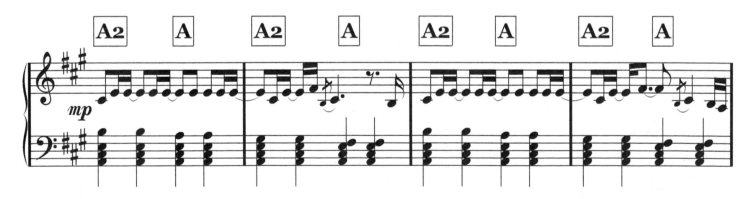

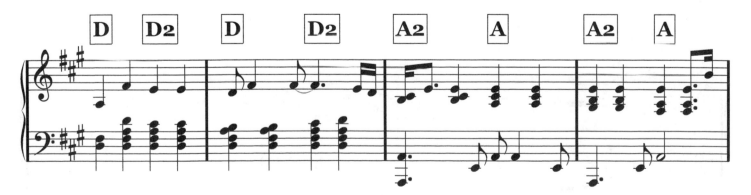

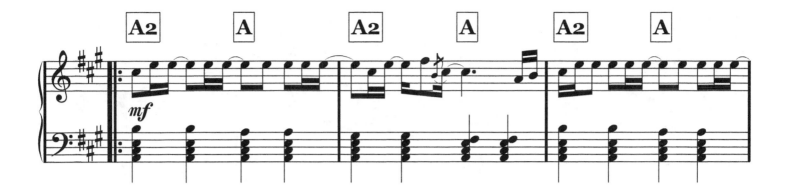

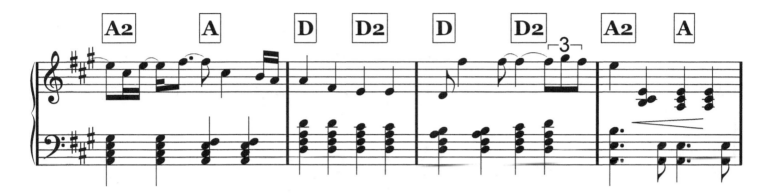

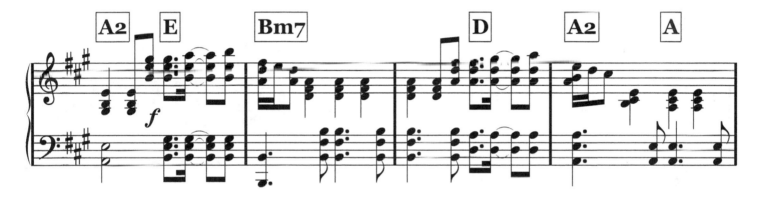

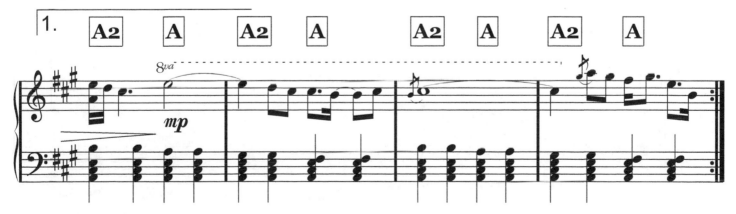

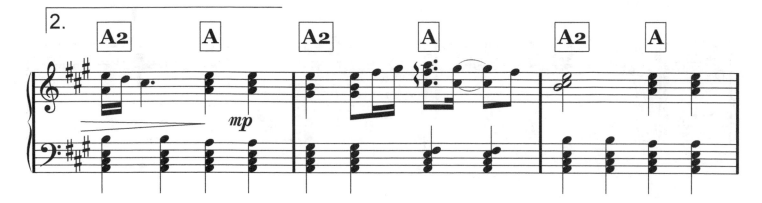

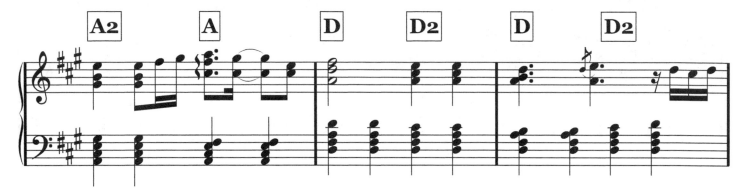

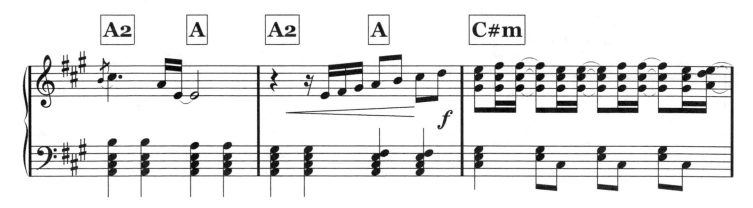

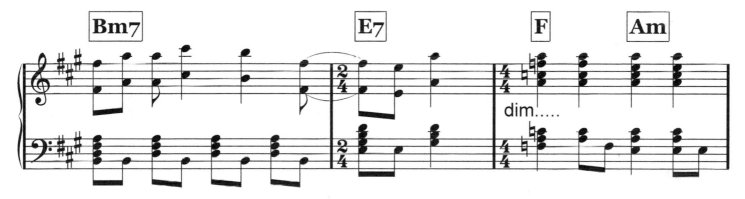

Sr. Troncoso

TRIANA

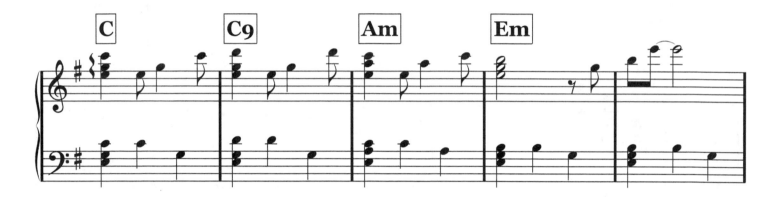

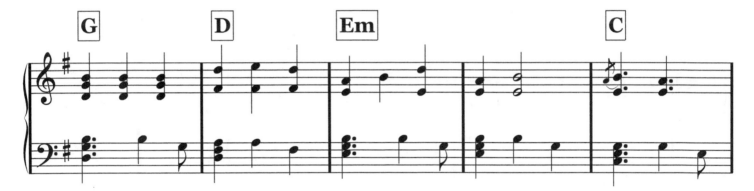

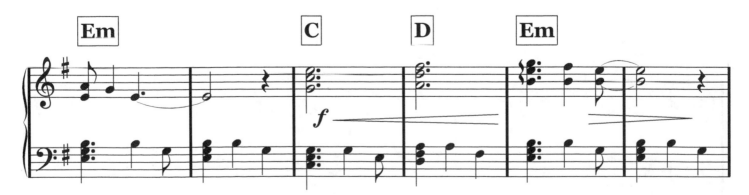

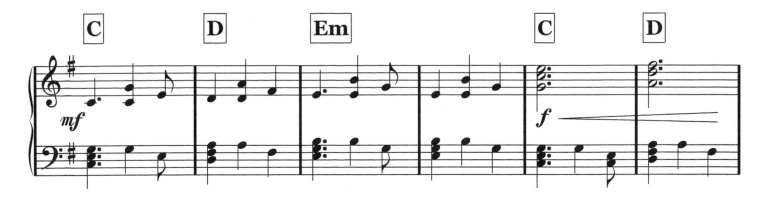

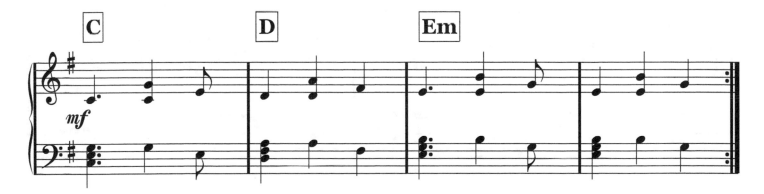

Dust in the Wind

KANSAS

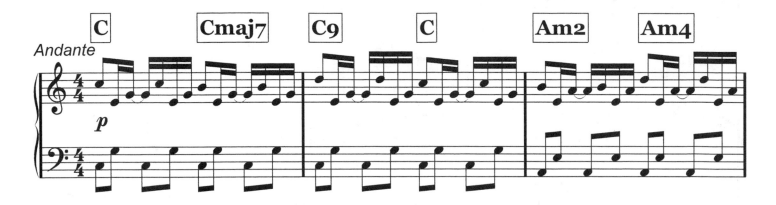

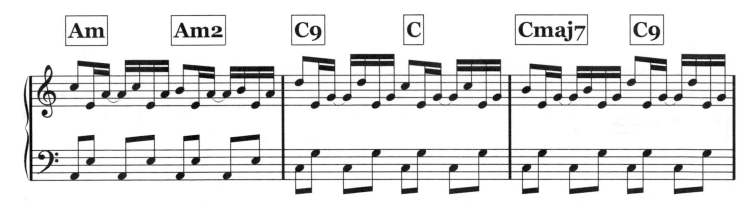

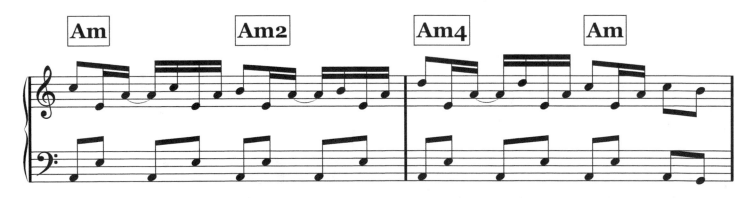

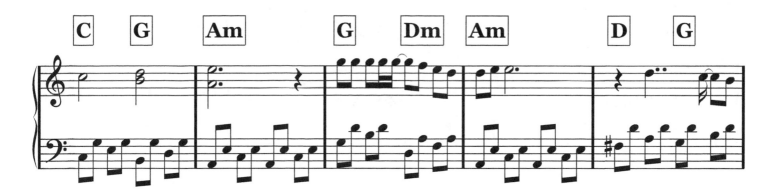

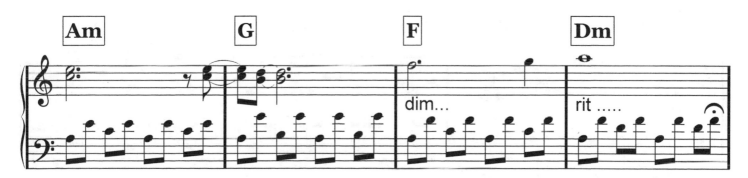

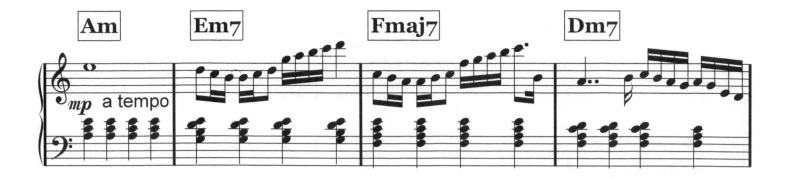

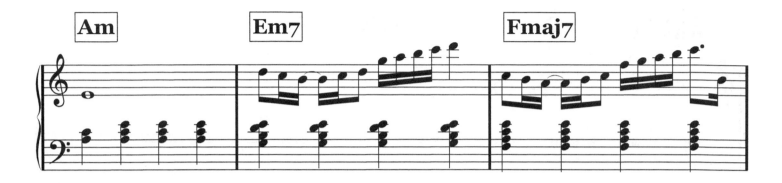

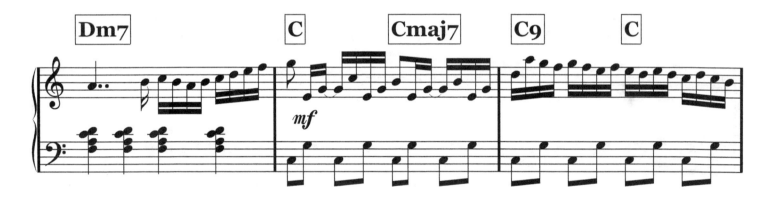

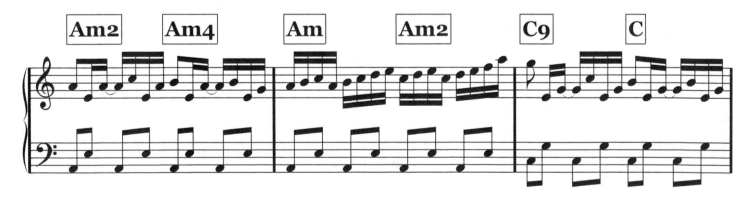

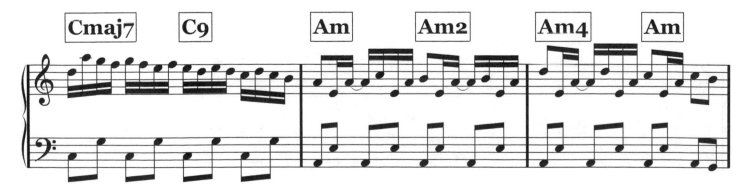

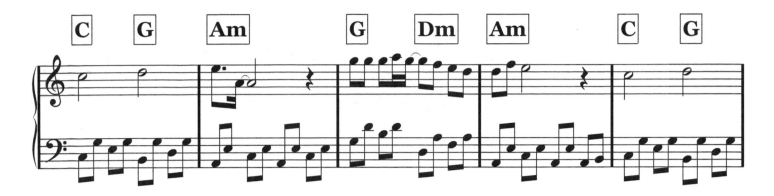

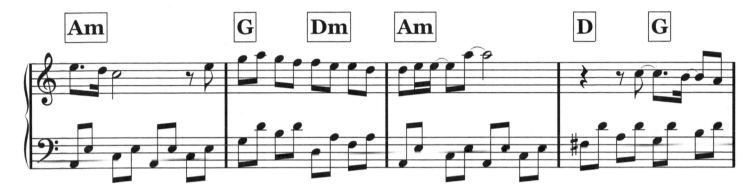

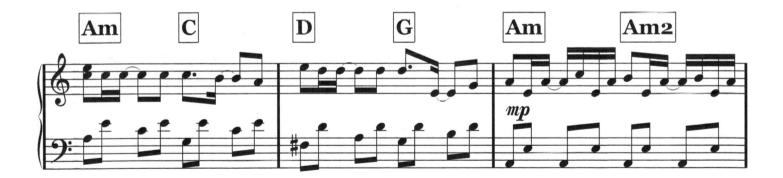

Mein Herz Brennt

RAMMSTEIN

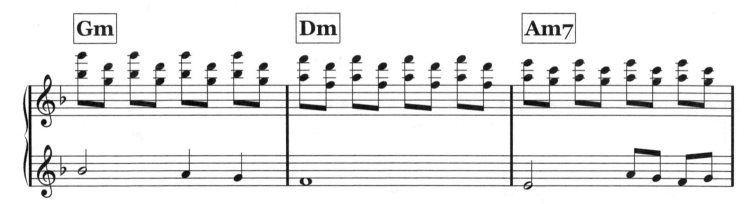

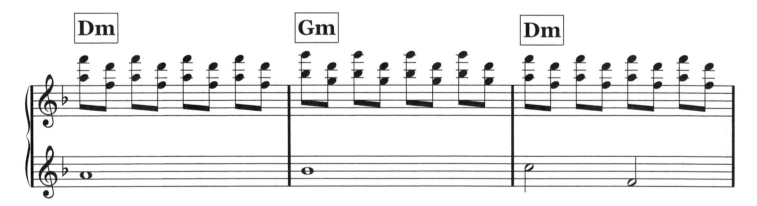

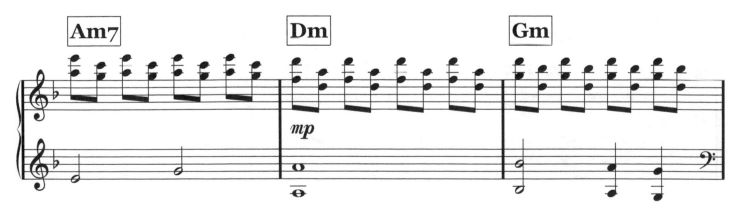

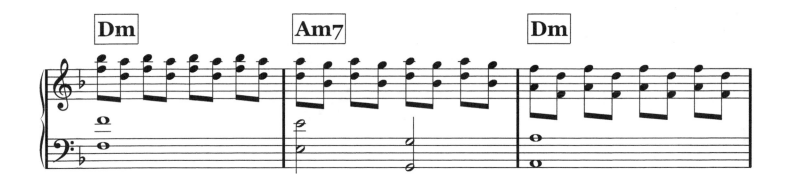

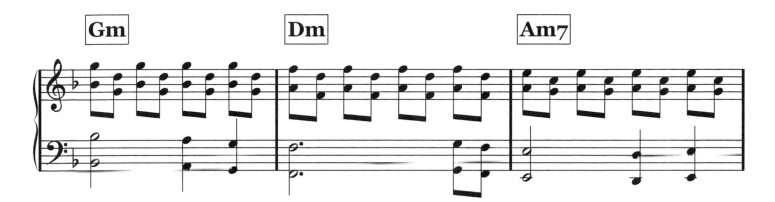

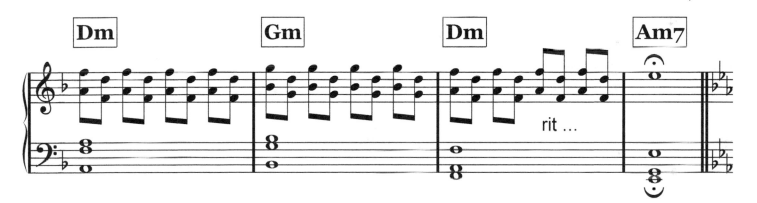

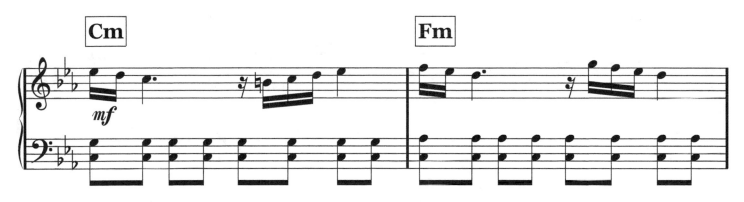

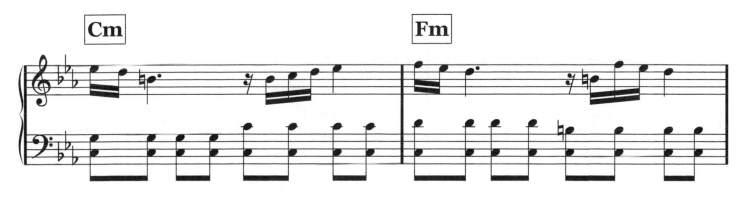

Cm

Cm   **Fm**

Ab   **G**   **Cm**

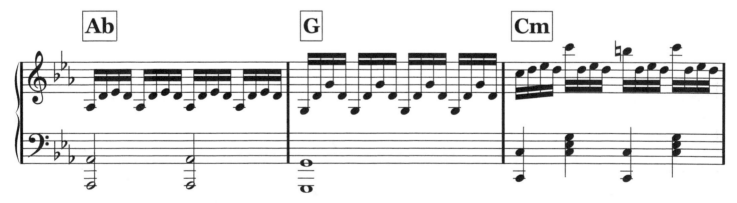

Fm   **Ab**   **G**

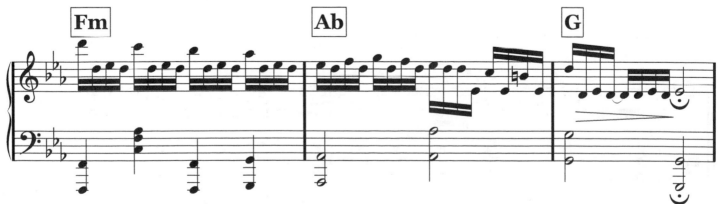

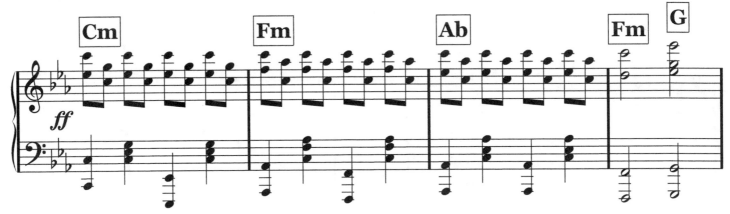

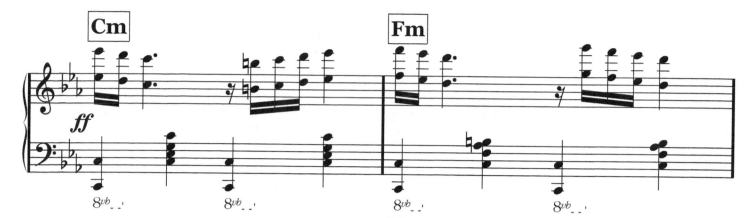

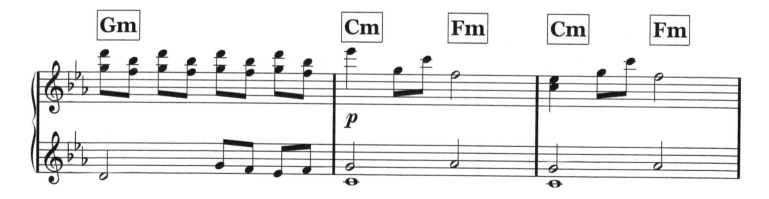

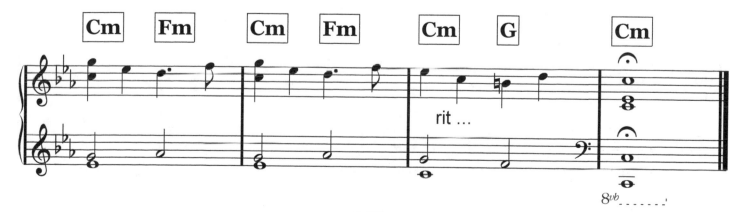

21st Century Schizoid Man

King Crimson

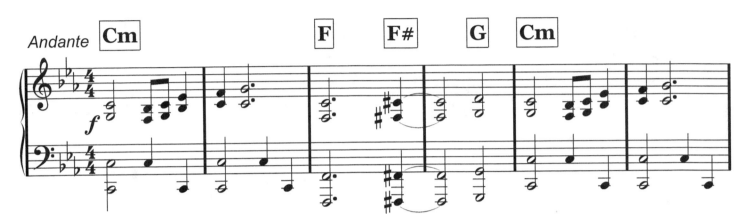

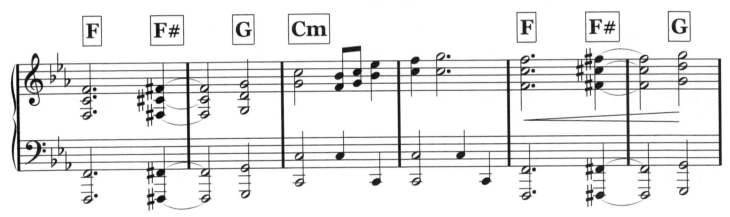

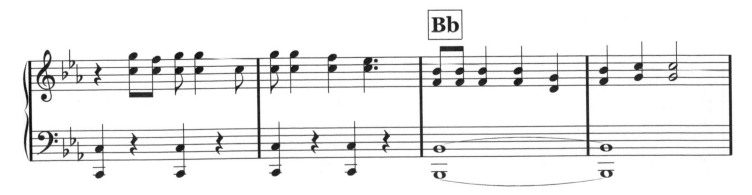

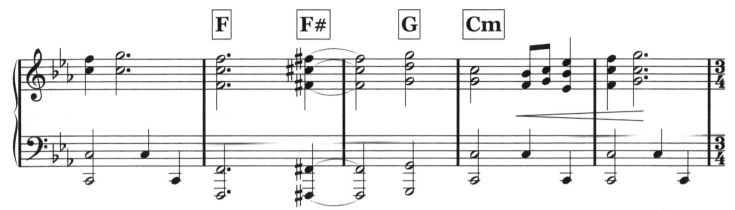

Cm

ff

Fm   Cm

Gm

mp

Long Distance Runaround
The Fish (Schindleria praematurus)
YES

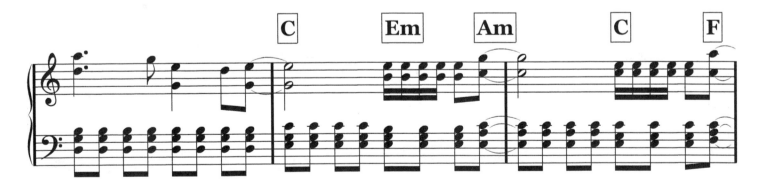

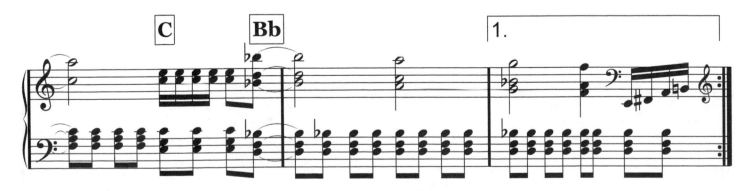

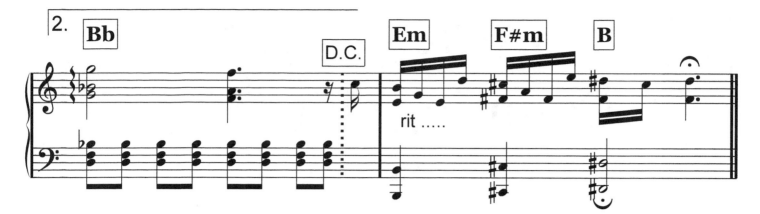

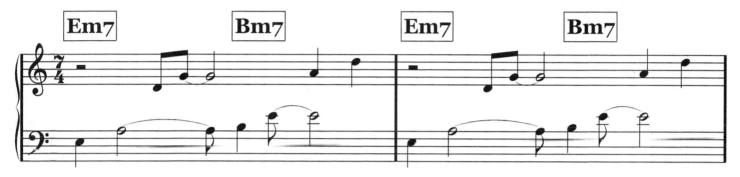

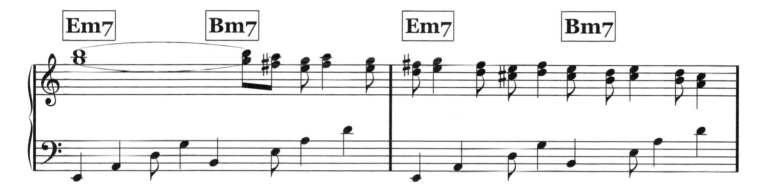

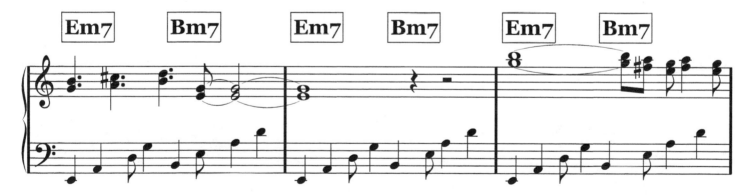

Hairless Heart
Counting Out Time
GENESIS

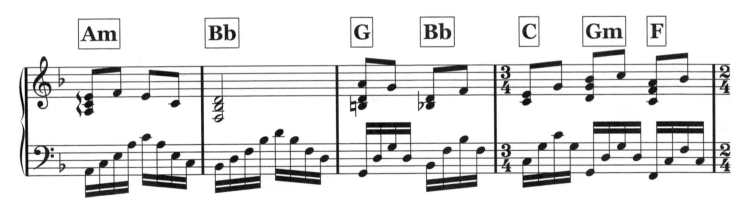

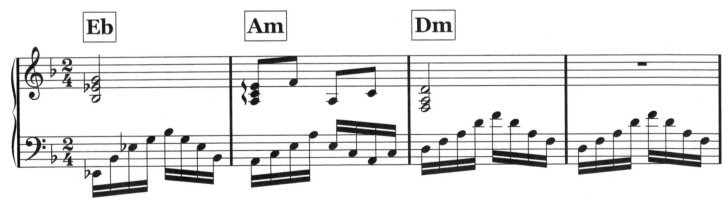

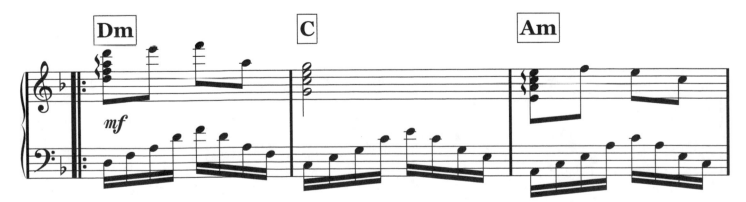

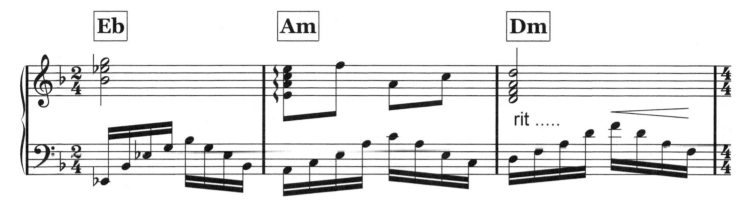

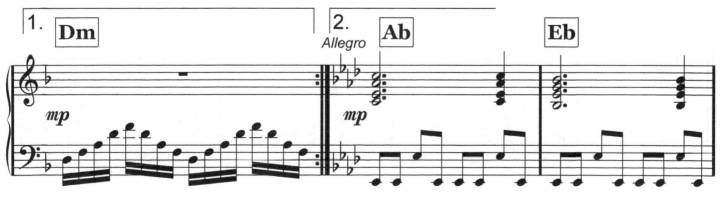

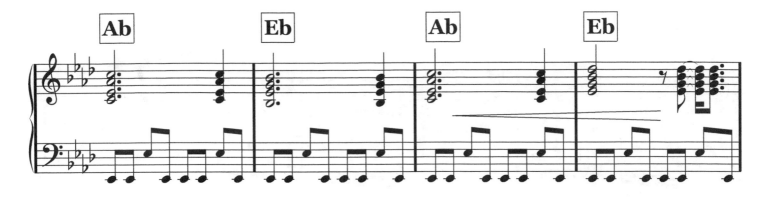

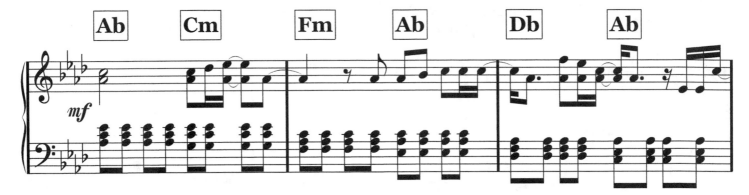

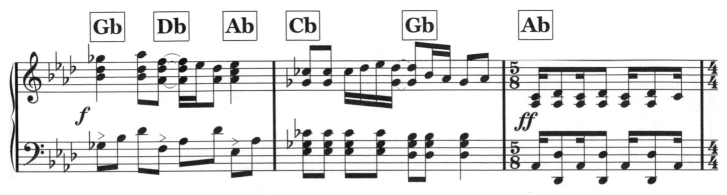

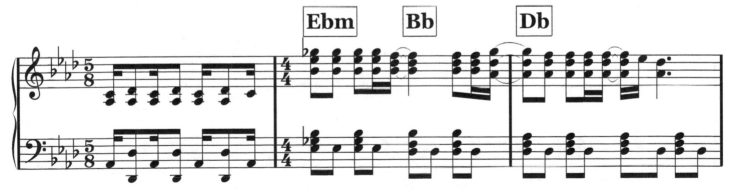

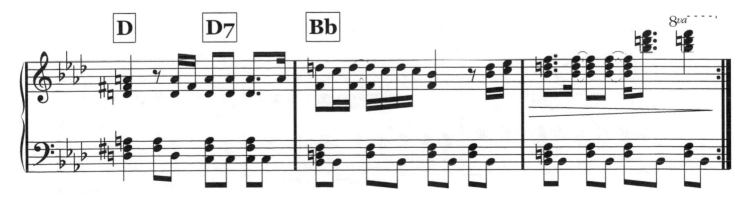

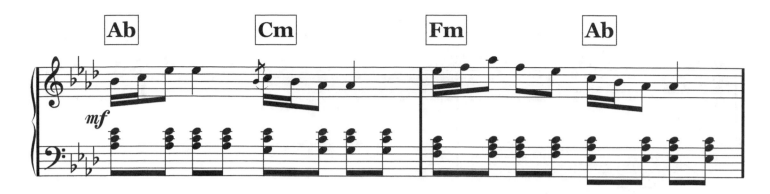

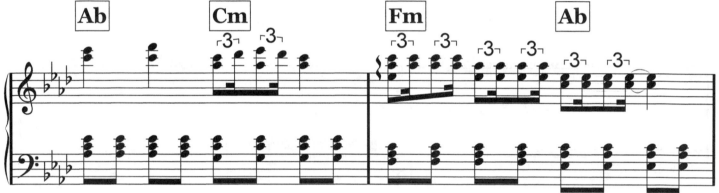

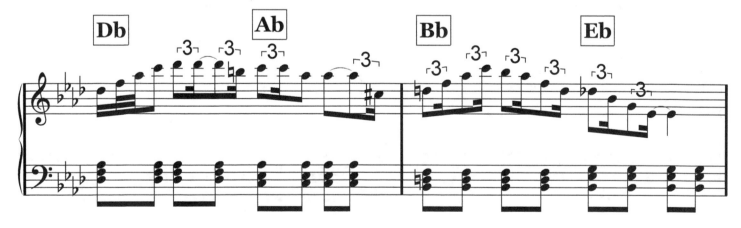

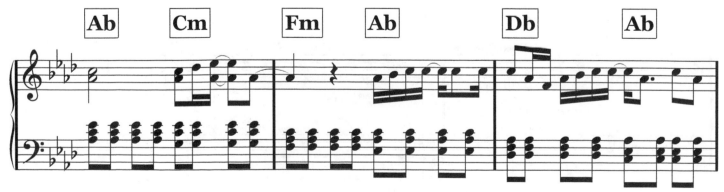

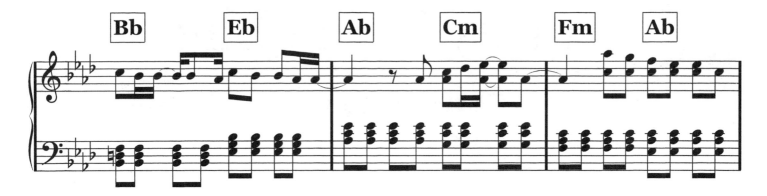

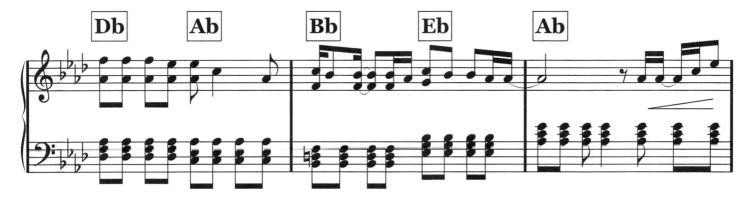

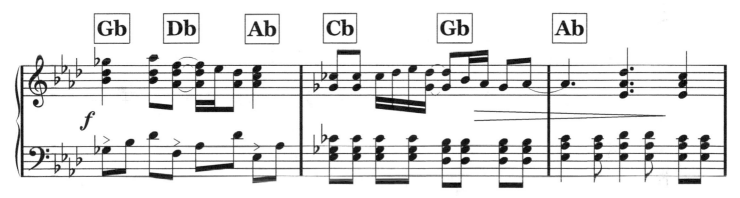

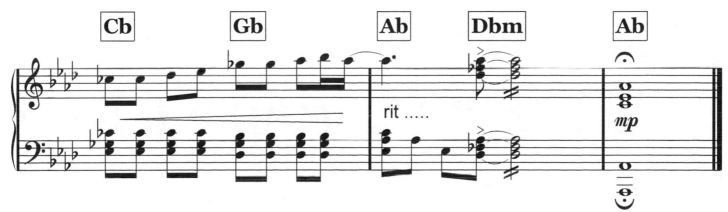

A Day in the Life

THE BEATLES

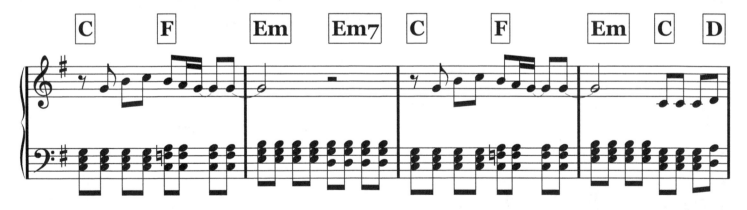

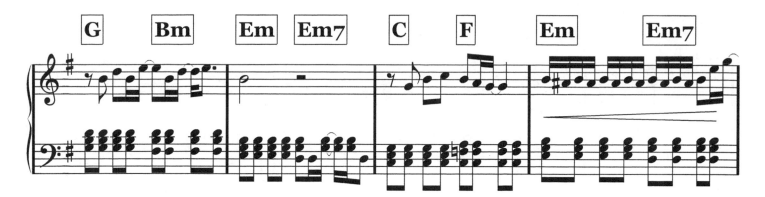

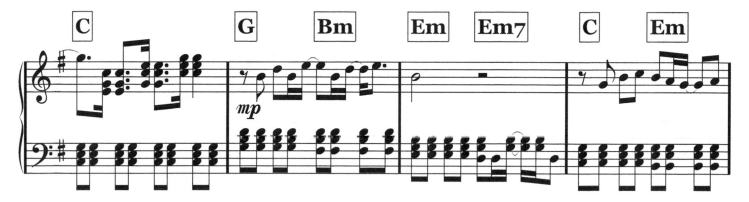

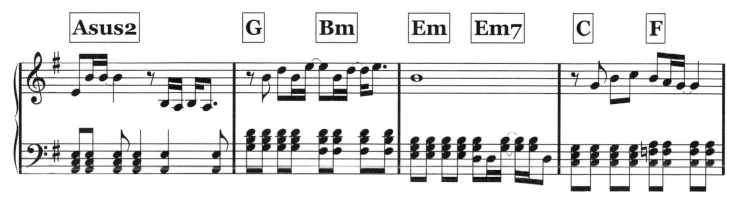

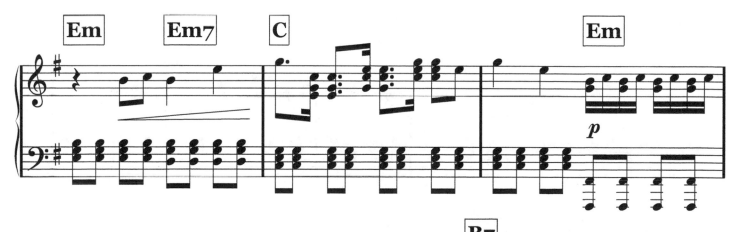

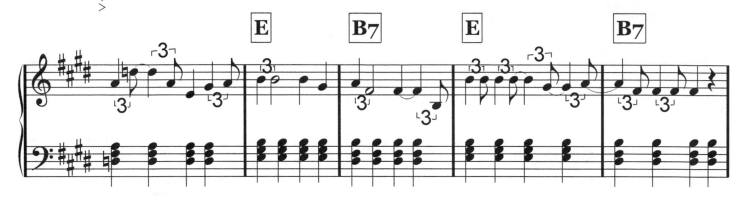

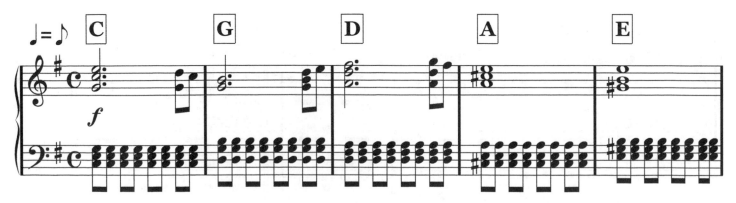

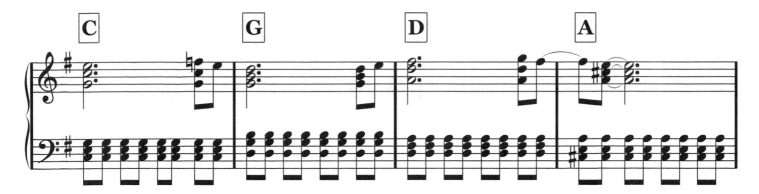

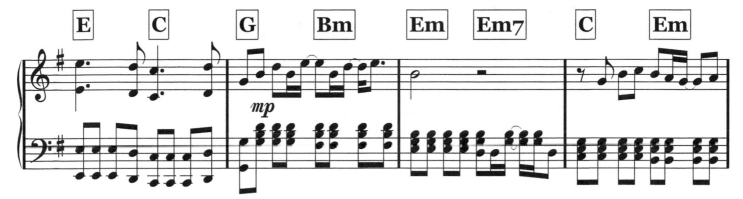

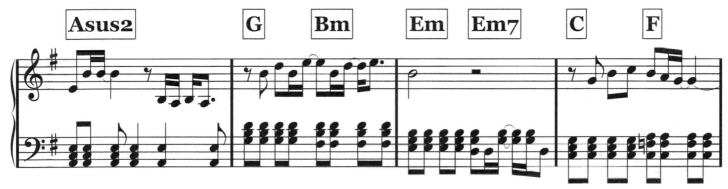

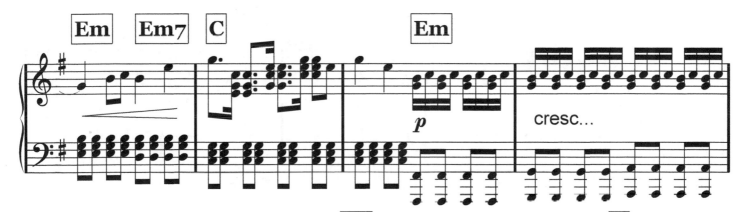

Fool´s Overture

SUPERTRAMP

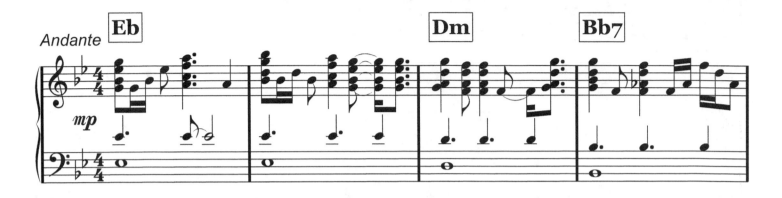

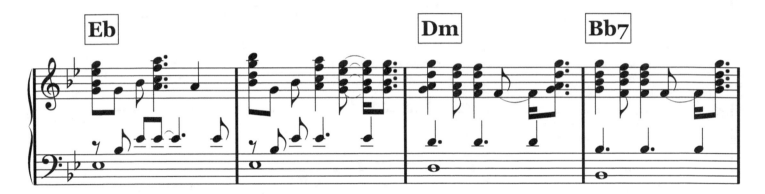

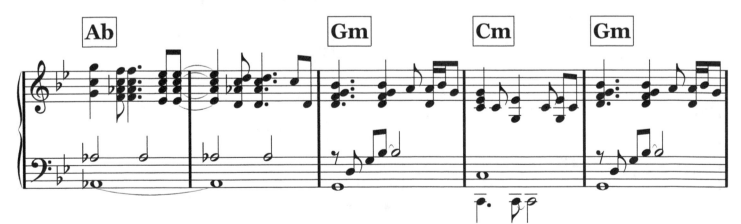

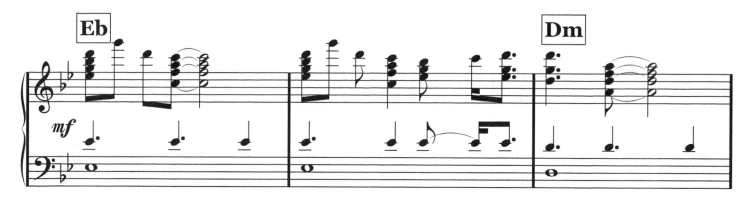

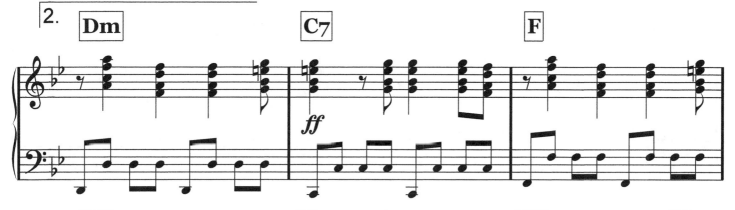

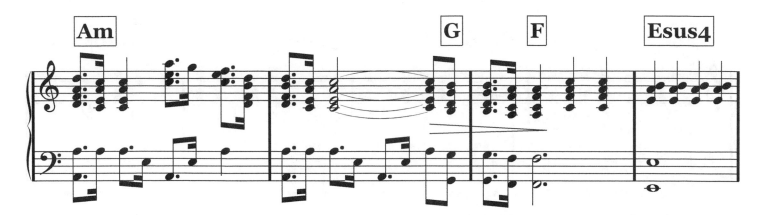

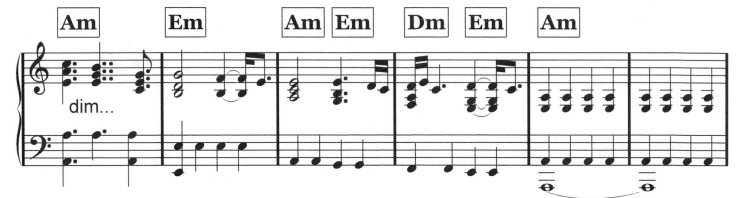

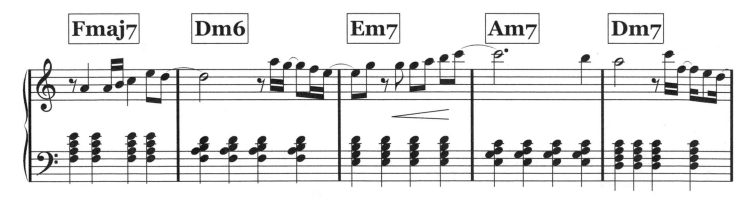

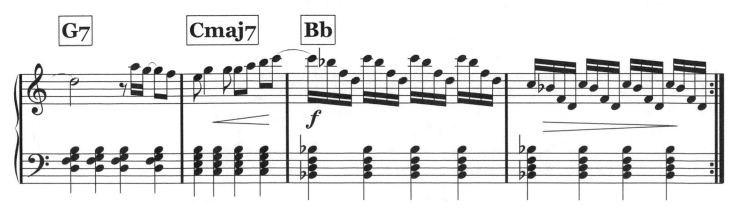

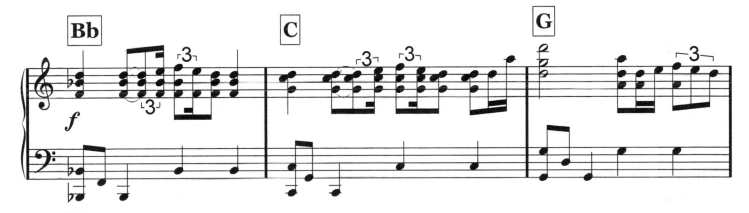

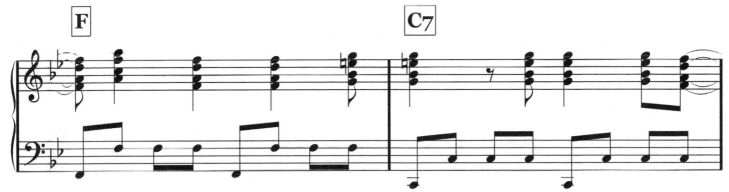

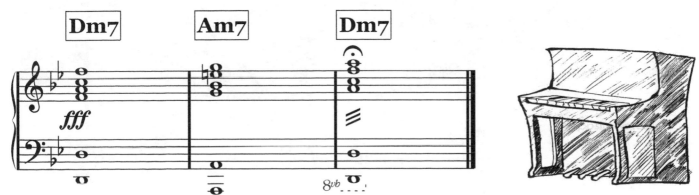